THE

QUARTERLY

EDITED BY

GORDON LISH

These dogs, they came from everywhere and there must have been a million of them. Much, much more than you could ever shake a stick at. I know—because I tried. I was using a stick to count them, and there were so many dogs, and I was getting so nervous, that my hand, and then the stick, were shaking. I counted 6,420 dogs. But don't hold me to that number. There was this one dog—I think I counted him twice.

—DOM LEONE, R.I.P.

Chip Kidd. Maybe you know the name Chip Kidd. Does our covers. Designs them, takes the pix that sort of roguely show up on them. Nice fellow. Wins awards all over the book biz for things he does—outsides of books, insides of books, the works. So the point is that he gets this bright idea, which is probably a pretty old-hat idea (or anyhow old-shirt idea). The difference is it's a Chip Kidd idea. Okay, so here's the story—you tell us you're willing to pledge yourself to fork over twenty-five bucks for one of these T-shirts of Chip's, which are, you know, Q T-shirts. So what we will then do, providing we get enough takers, is this—hustle up some T-shirtmaker to make. Your shirt and everybody else's. Which (you can't tell from this drawing guess-who has done, but who is stopping you from using your imagination?) is going to have our logo on the front in white (the color of the T-shirt, right?) against a block of color right out of a dream. Sort of rosey-ish but lurider. Plus our banner line—which, in case you don't know what a banner line is, is THE QUARTERLY IS. And on the back? What goes on the back? Because that's the answer—WHAT. Like this—WHAT? With a question mark, just the way that that was. Now, what do you do to put us on notice? Here is another answer. A note to the editor. It says *Kidd's Shirt*—and follows with your name and address.

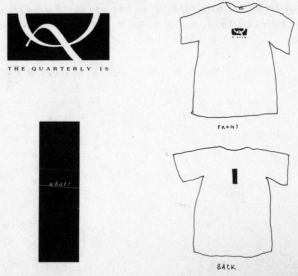

THE
QUARTERLY

17 / SPRING 1991

VINTAGE BOOKS

A DIVISION OF RANDOM HOUSE, INC.

NEW YORK

THE QUARTERLY (ISSN: 0893-3103) IS EDITED BY GORDON LISH
AND IS PUBLISHED MARCH, JUNE, SEPTEMBER, AND DECEMBER AT
201 EAST 50TH STREET, NEW YORK, NY 10022. SUBSCRIPTIONS—
FOUR ISSUES AT $40 US, $54 CANADIAN, $46 US OVERSEAS—AND ADDRESS
CHANGES SHOULD BE SENT TO THE ATTENTION OF SUBSCRIPTION OFFICE,
28TH FLOOR. ORDERS RECEIVED BY JANUARY 31 START WITH MARCH NUMBER;
BY APRIL 30, JUNE NUMBER; BY JULY 31, SEPTEMBER NUMBER; BY OCTOBER 31,
DECEMBER NUMBER. SEE LAST PAGE FOR PURCHASE OF BACK NUMBERS.

MANAGEMENT BY ELLEN F. TORRON
EDITORIAL ASSISTANCE BY RICK WHITAKER

THE QUARTERLY WELCOMES THE OPPORTUNITY TO READ WORK OF EVERY
CHARACTER, AND IS ESPECIALLY CONCERNED TO KEEP ITSELF AN OPEN FORUM.
MANUSCRIPTS MUST BE ACCOMPANIED BY THE CUSTOMARY RETURN MATERIALS, AND
SHOULD BE ADDRESSED TO THE EDITOR. *THE QUARTERLY* MAKES THE UTMOST
EFFORT TO OFFER ITS RESPONSE TO MANUSCRIPTS NO LATER THAN ONE WEEK
SUBSEQUENT TO RECEIPT. OPINIONS EXPRESSED HEREIN ARE NOT NECESSARILY
THOSE OF THE EDITOR OR OF THE PUBLISHER.

ISBN: 0-679-73494-5

DESIGN BY ANDREW ROBERTS
ADVERTISING MANAGEMENT BY DAVID S. W. SCHAB
INSTALLATION BY DENISE STEWART

THE HOB BROUN PRIZE FOR 1990 IS AWARDED TO MELINDA DAVIS FOR HER Q14
FICTIONS "THIS IS THE STORY" AND "TEXT." Q READERS ARE REMINDED THAT
THE PRIZE WAS ESTABLISHED BY MR. AND MRS. HEYWOOD HALE BROUN IN
MEMORY OF THEIR SON, AND THAT IT IS AWARDED ANNUALLY TO A WRITER WHOSE
WORK IN FICTION EXHIBITS EXCEPTIONAL DARING AND GRACE. ON ANOTHER
POINT—HEAVEN KNOWS, WE ARE A LITTLE MAGAZINE AND THEREFORE OUGHT NOT
TO REQUIRE THE LABORS OF VERY MANY PEOPLE FOR US TO KEEP PRESENTING
OURSELVES TO THE VERY MANY PEOPLE WHO HAVE COME TO BE OUR READERS.
BUT THE HORRID TRUTH IS THAT A HORDE OF ABLE HANDS MUST CONSPIRE
ONE WITH ANOTHER FOR THIS SMALL ENTERPRISE TO FLOURISH—
TO BE SURE, TOO LARGE A HORDE FOR *THE QUARTERLY*'S MASTHEAD TO BEAR
THE MANYNESS THEREOF. BUT FROM TIME TO TIME IT IS ENTIRELY POSSIBLE AND
CORRECT FOR THERE TO BE AN ACCOUNTING MADE, THIS WITH THE STATEMENT OF
THANKS THAT IS OWED. VERY WELL, THEN—THANK YOU, THANK YOU, TO ALL
THE FOLLOWING: KAREN SMITH, HAROLD VAUGHN, LINDA ROSENBERG,
PHILLIP CICIONE, GEORGE DONAHUE, LYNN WARSHOW, SUSAN GROARKE,
SYBIL PINCUS, PETER ANDERSEN, IRENA VUKOV-KENDES, LAUREN EMERSON,
AND REBECCA AIDLIN.

THE QUARTERLY

17 / SPRING 1991

THE QUARTERLY

HOORAY FOR YANNICK MURPHY, MARK RICHARD, AND D. NURSKE, ALL, GOD LOVE US, QUARTERLIERS, AND ALL, GOD LOVE THEM, RECIPIENTS OF $30,000 GRANTS FROM THE WHITING FOUNDATION. AND HUZZAH FOR TED PEJOVICH, PETER CHRISTOPHER, AND WILLIAM TESTER, ALSO OFTEN AT THIS ADDRESS, ON WHOSE WALLETS THE NATIONAL ENDOWMENT FOR THE ARTS HAS SMILED.

THE
QUARTERLY

Cruise

The day Sean shot Theresa and killed their baby I was on a boat cruise with Jennifer steaming across a glassy wide-open bay to a seafood restaurant on the other side. Jennifer was wearing a deep blue cocktail dress and looked about as pretty as I'd ever seen her. She had bad skin but her face was well formed and curvy and her eyes were nice. I hadn't laid a hand on her up until this cruise, and even on the smooth ferryboat trip I thought little of touching her. I was leaving to go back to school in another state, and it was enough being with her up until I left.

Sean shot Theresa in her sleep, with a pistol, a nine-millimeter Beretta replica made in Brazil. No one had had any indication that this would happen: he was sane—a college graduate. He shot her through the back about nine times. It was exactly nine times. He told me later he heard her moaning and gurgling for a little while after he shot her, like she was having an extremely bad dream. A very, very bad dream. He told me the blood was deep.

As Sean said this, I thought about how speedy little nine-millimeter bullets go right through a body, letting it live for a while, whereas a .45 bullet would have pushed big holes into a human form, stomping the life out of it.

After he shot Theresa, Sean crawled to the other side of the bed to watch her die, and he looked at her brown eyes going fishy and soft, and he felt nothing for her, he said, nothing.

I never liked Theresa.

"You don't just shoot someone like that for no reason," I said to Sean. "No reason."

He agreed. He knew he needed to have a reason, it was just that he couldn't think of any at the time. He said he'd get back to me: "I'll get back to you" were his words, without a trace of irony.

"And what about the baby?" I asked.

"What about it?" he replied. Irony this time.

Jennifer had sat on the bench of the ferry, letting the salty air breathe through her hair, across her face. Her skin looked a little oily. I mentioned before she had bad skin; I am mentioning it again. Blue eyes, but bad skin. She was twenty-four years old, like Sean and me. Theresa was twenty-one. Jennifer's body was too thin, from career worries. But pretty. A face that would have been gorgeous asleep, at rest. An unhappy expression. Vacuous. But pretty. I wanted to sleep with her, I really did. I just couldn't work up the lust.

I was with Sean when he bought the Beretta about three years ago. This was out of college. He came back from Wharton Business School in Pennsylvania to live in California, where we grew up, near the beach. His parents were disappointed that he came back. Sean and I lived together in a too-expensive, two-bedroom, one-bath condo near the beach. In the morning and at dusk we walked to the beach and swam in the ocean. During the day I went to college and he worked programming computers. At night sometimes we drove to a record store to buy compact disks (we bought our CD players together, at a discount) or we went shooting. He was a terrible shot.

He made $30,000 a year, which seemed like a lot of money, so he bought a new IBM PC and a motorcycle and a Beretta nine-millimeter which was really made by a company in Brazil. I was a student and had substantially less money than he did, so he lent me $286 to buy a Colt .45 replica. I still have that gun. It sits loaded next to my bedside, the bullets waiting like little old friends.

Once Jennifer wanted me to kiss her, I could tell, but we were just friends, you know, happy hours together after school, renting videos, not really anything meaningful. Sean had found Theresa, who was short, fat, and ugly, but he had what he wanted, which was someone who would be there no matter how big a dump he took on her. He did treat her well, up until he shot her. He even kissed her in public, which is pretty amazing for Sean.

I took Jennifer shooting once. She was a good shot; she had an eye for it. She didn't like the people at the gun club: they made her nervous. I told her they were just people, everyday folks.

One day after he and Theresa started sleeping together a lot, Sean was getting up out of bed when Theresa grabbed his ear and tweaked it "hard," he said, for a joke. Out of reflex, he slapped her. "Really hard," he said. He had this thing where when he was really hungry he'd get furious. It's like when we were living together; on Sunday mornings he'd leave me behind to go get breakfast if I wasn't ready, and we'd eat separately. But he was always nice and apologetic after he ate and came back.

Theresa got pregnant about two months after they started regularly sleeping together. She was so ugly, always puffy, almost like a sumo wrestler, and she had the soft kind of skin that bruised easily. She had vitamin deficiencies. I hated even looking at her. I'd have to psych myself up. I'd say to myself, "Maybe she isn't that bad, maybe she isn't . . ." and I'd look and she was. Every time she was.

Jennifer and I had classes together. Two years ago I introduced her to Sean, who was my roommate at the time. He went after her right away, but she didn't like him because he wasn't forceful enough. This was about two years ago. We've been friends ever since. That is, Jennifer, Sean, and I.

Sean and I grew up together. We saw our first porn together, witnessed each other falling in love. I told myself it's what friends share.

I started seeing Jennifer in a different light, once it was established that I was leaving to go to school far away. Things had that odd finality between us, and it felt like a deal ready to be closed. But Sean always said I wasn't a closer.

Sean wouldn't talk about Theresa's pregnancy. I'd go to his parents' house to work on my car when Sean would be there, and no one ever said anything about it. Once I asked him and he said, "I try not to think about it." He laughed like it was a joke, which I think it was, so I laughed too. Everyone thought Theresa trapped him because she was so ugly and he had so much, being a Wharton graduate and everything.

They had to induce labor; the baby didn't want to come. Sean called me from the hospital. He told me they'd just given her drugs. "She's throwing up," he said, sounding very far away, like the announcer reporting the Hindenburg disaster. I expected him to say, "The humanity, the humanity . . ."

The three of them lived in Sean's one-bedroom apartment. He moved his comic book collections and old calculus textbooks to the garage downstairs. The crib stayed in the master bedroom, at the foot of their queen-size bed. After he shot Theresa, he took a knife and stabbed the baby, "over and over," he said. Those were the words he used, "over and over." I think it bears repeating.

Every night before I went to sleep I thought about holding Jennifer, breathing quietly into her hair, into the back of her neck. Then I thought about what I had to do with my life in the morning. Then I went back to Jennifer, but by then I was asleep and coasting into a dream.

Whenever we got together, Sean said it was like a yuppie TV show. I did not feel that way. I had movement in my life. I was going to graduate school on the East Coast. Sean bought things steadily—a big-screen TV and a really nice VCR with four heads. Both with remote control.

When we were on the ferry going to the seafood restaurant, I thought very briefly of pushing Jennifer overboard. You know—a joke: a push. Very briefly. Then the boat's whistle screamed and I turned away from her to watch as we approached the dock of the seafood restaurant. The wind coming off the bay felt sticky and good. I reminded myself one more time—it was just a joke, just to myself. **Q**

Pumping Gas for Hemingway

Like I said, a regular day, slumped in this very same chair, swatting bottle flies big as your nose, and wishing like hell for AC—no different from all the other days I pumped, 365 a year. Now, I'm talking about my meeting Hemingway. I've been talking about my meeting him for a good while and it begins to tire me. Ernst, I said to him off the cuff and he corrected: Ernest.

This is not a Hemingway story. If it were, I'd not have much to say. As it is, there's little enough. A little's a lot in his hands—though surely the flesh on his hands has withered, dust to dust, while my hands here, stained as they are, continue honest toil: pumping gas, dipping oil, swatting bottle flies. Hell, my hands still work my wife's body, bless her, though not as usual as we used to. God knows, hard as we tried, we weren't blessed with the expected prodigy and no doctor has yet explained to us why. The Lord works for Himself and I'm not setting this out as a complaint against Him. No. But frankly, and you're probably too young to appreciate this thought, you take away the mystery of the seed's conception and you take away a little from the tumble's luster. I remember my father's first car, a Model T—Mr. Ford made as many as there are bees in summer—and when he drove it toward our house, rattling and farting, for the family's initial look-see, I took off for the backwoods, where I lasted with the sunlight. Afterward, once I'd become familiar with the Model T's noise, you couldn't keep me from under its hood. It wasn't long before the Ford's mysteries didn't hide themselves, the crankshaft and mechanics not much different from my rubber-band-propelled balsa-wood planes. And then I wasn't frightened and could ignore that monster, though I realize now that my skill with cars comes from that need to know. The knowing comes easy, that's why you and me are here.

So, getting back to the point of all this, if this was a Hemingway story, we'd have a real short story. Still might. I'm beginning to tire.

I don't see why, once and for all, you can't just copy it right.

I read a book of his about fishing and hunting—two things I know a little about. Filled, too, with wars and bullfights. If I remember, one of them stories was called A Short Story or A Very Short Story or A Little Story, just leaving out the words like *True* or *Romance* or *Murder* that'd make you want to pick it up for a read. So if this was Hemingway's story, it might already be over. We'd stand each other drinks—I keep a little flask under my ledger in the cash drawer—talk rough, in the fewest possible words, and maybe get blustery under influence of the liquor, relate a tall tale or two, and I would have stopped already. Throw my grease-stained hands in the air and shout, "Enough!" Might even throw a greasy hand at your eye if you looked wrongly at me.

This is the truth, my meeting Hemingway on a regular day.

A real meeting.

A regular guy.

Once I got jocular—just a wild hair, hell, I might never see the fella again, I might not see nobody except maybe them state politicians troop in every even year or so with them pie-in-the-sky plans no Jack could ever stick their thumb into. Might not see nobody but them, excepting, of course—and I'm not slighting them, mind you, but them I see every day—the folks about here, the ones that stay loyal to me, that is, and don't drive over to that spanking new dinosaur off the inner-state trying to take my business—once, like I said, I felt this wild hair and said Ernst and he looked fit to be tied, kind of set his face, but fella he needed gas, probably didn't realize he had gas aplenty to get out of these sticks and into his kind of society. "Ernest," he said.

It was the first time I'd met him.
He needed gas.
I could oblige.

Heat about as bad as today's. You might be thinking with all that sweat soaking into your shirt that this place of mine could use a little modernizing, and I'll grant you that; it does need something. Business is no longer the same, and I'm not getting younger.

You've a wife? I love mine, you write that part down, but the truth, for your ears and education only, not for front-page gossip, is that a woman ain't never satisfied with what a man gives her. Just when you think you done right by her, she lets loose with something makes your heart jump. I sometimes think about those bugs making dinner of their mates after the humping and wonder if we've developed much further.

Take Hemingway. I've done some reading and learned, sure enough, he had four women tell him "I do." Four. And him a fine figure, with his hefty size, looking a little lopsided the year I saw him, off balance, like his inner ear weren't functioning like it should, or like all the words he'd written were a screen against everything the world might want to say to help. Reminds me of a lady around here used to be the county's best source of doings, taking in everyone's troubles and then passing them along over cards and church bingo. Now all she's good for is her own muddled story. The banks that held those other lives gave way and the stories she heard and told all her life now mix together with her own, and it's all your memory can handle to decide if she was the one blocking the courthouse in '67, or was it Mrs. Elmira White, as your papers reported.

But Hemingway, you ask. I was surprised to see him in my part of Florida. I'm orange-grove country, clapboard-house country, church at every street corner, few streets and corners there are, Friday-night bingo, revival country. Why am I wasting breath talking about that? Hell, you can look out and witness. Across the road there, see that bit of—what do your papers call it? Shanty, yes. Lloyd Tucker's place. His wife ran off with the spiritualist after talking with her first husband's vision. Crops been rotting on the trees since. Now they don't even fruit except these stunted bitter things no bigger than berries. Lloyd lost the punch or whatever. Folks say he'll wander his groves at night, no stitch of clothing, and that's the only attention he pays them, if that. You know Hemingway could make a reason for it, sure. Let me get back to the meeting.

Here he was in that fine black Caddy of his, old fin model, sweating a bit in the sun, jumping out of the door before I can get up to it. I didn't know it was him, right off. Hadn't the pleasure of meeting before. He stood tall, sweating in the heat, swatting at a bottle fly same as you now. Asked for Regular. I said to him, after I'd taken a good squint while I tanked his car, I said, Say, you know you look kinda like that writer fella, and he said, Yeah? Who's that? Guy got that foreign peace prize few years back, I said to him. He said, Yeah?

We may look backwoods, but I keep up on the news. Nice TV my wife and I watch from bed. This station, you've probably noticed, doesn't take much of my time, sad to say, so our weekly paper usually gets a pretty fair shake. I'm looking at his sweat, looking at the car. Couldn't be, I'm telling myself. You get into these patterns, routines: open at seven, service the few regulars stop in, worry your head and laugh at the sin Charlie recounts to you on his mail break (the doings people write!), close at six. Then it's a walk home to the wife: dinner, TV, sleep. You see the same folks day in, day out. Talk about the fishing and how the birds are flying, though I'm not much inclined that way these days. The occasional tourists that wing our way just drive straight through our country, nothing really to stop for, but everybody from these parts enjoys catching the news from Jesse.

Here. I'm going on again. I'm here to tell you my Hemingway story and it keeps getting away from me. God, I'm tired. Late, I suppose.

Age, then. Age will do it.

I liked him. His car. The look of him in his smart clothes, white collar open at his tanned neck. I liked his fussiness when I called him by name and he told me, No, it was two syllables, for Christ's sake, not a one-syllable name. How would I know different? I'm a gasser. I pumped gas for Hemingway.

He asked if it was good in these parts. I said sure, there's hunting. I told him about the brake he'd passed about three miles back the road he'd driven, true for a shot or two right time of year. We chatted easy like that, me trying to put that picture straight out of my mind, simple as you please, leisurely as if he stopped in every day to catch the news with Jesse.

Okay. I'll say this short because I'm getting pretty tired and this scene bothers me.

When I was a kid, my brother and I hunted with our father every chance we could. My father enjoyed our company and our work. He used us as his retrievers because our dogs always mangled the birds. Chewed them good. Boy, my father'd kick into them. You'd think they'd have learned, but they never really did. Maybe their breeding. Lack of. Maybe it was that blood on their tongue setting them afire for a real swizzle.

What I'm fixing to say worries me still, but I'll go on with it since I've started.

Once the three of us—Dad, Jacob (my brother), and I—tracked to this barbwire fence, not far from that brake. My father had the gun, so he ducked under the wire first. Jacob held the top wire to give my father a little extra help getting through so he wouldn't tangle and lash us with his tongue. I don't remember exactly what I was doing, but I recollect an urge to wizz soon as I could.

I'm no storyteller. You see it already.

Birds flushed from a cover to the side of me, and I whistled for my father's attention. The gun rang, Jacob yelled—these two together. My ears were ringing like I'd been palm-clapped in a fight, so I couldn't hear much of anything, and what I began to see didn't appear real. What soon lay before me looked like a scene on the other side of a glass panel, like big saltwater fish in those huge glass aquariums at the marina, true to life if you fell alongside their supper into the tank with them, but standing on dry tile merely gawking outside what you hope is sturdy glass, they're images like on a TV screen.

The birds had continued winging into the sky. I turned. My father had a hand at his hair, one foot caught in the wire, staring behind him toward where Jacob should be standing.

Why didn't I see that first?

I looked at the ground, having forgotten him in the confusion of birds and shots—lost game—but now I knew I was about to see something important, something that would stay with me to this very minute—and there, on the ground, Jacob, kind of twisted, twitching like a clipped bird, face gone.

I had a few stories I wanted to tell Hemingway, a few I thought he'd want to write, but I kept them to myself. I kind of hoped he might tell me a story or two while I rubbed the bugs best I could from the windshield. He stood there and wiped his neck with a good cloth handkerchief.

Used to hanker toward writing myself. More after I met the man. You, now, probably have some fancy education, lots of book learning. You studied your business. Well, I never studied much on writing, but talking comes easy enough to me, to all of us here. It's all we got. Understand? No modern libraries, no state universities. Not even a community college. We're regular folks, friends and enemies, as soon pass gossip as piss.

For instance, if this was a true Hemingway story, which it is, mind you, but in a different way, hell, we'd be through.

We ought to work this thing over and be done with it.

Here.

Charged him two dollars for the gas. His oil was good and running smooth, almost no clotting. Tugged at his belts and they held firm. A man who cared for his car. So that was that. Gave me a fiver, returned three ones, and he said good day. Same to you, I said. I believe I told him to pass our way again.

Waited out that day in my office, tired as I am now, then closed a bit early if I recollect.

At home, I washed and sat at the table. Margaret served me ham and runners from our garden. I told her about my day, about meeting this writer fella. That's nice, she said. I tried to tell her about him and she said to eat her cooking before it cooled. I remember a few days later driving over to the city library—a fair haul—and finding that book with the hunting and fishing stories. Guys drinking. Seemed like he had some mean things against the war, but hell, I'd seen him, looked American enough, but for a time or two I wondered if I'd pumped a commie. Showed the book to Margaret, pointed to his picture, and she nodded her stitch into her fabric. Didn't faze her at all, and I kept on with the excitement of it, playing that meeting in my mind every time I bought and read another of his books, wondering if he'd ever stop by again and take up with me. You know, we'd pal around these parts. He'd show me his deep-sea rigs. We'd jaw some. I thought these things for years. Even through the night I come home from here and Margaret said, that writer fella (and she thumbed her place in the pages and flipped to his grizzled face on the dust jacket), she said, that writer fella you got so hepped over went and shot himself. He don't like women much, do he? she said, and then easy as you please returned to her reading. Kissed his life good-bye. And that took some thinking. Him, a writer, more famous than our damn politicians, and something about his life wasn't right. I puzzled it. Woman trouble? Too easy. I pondered what kind of story might be in his death. And then I wondered if I'd actually told him about my brother Jacob, told him without my remembering. What lessons were in this for Jesse. . . .

You—listen. You'll say what I didn't. When you write this, I'll sound like a yammering old fool. I'll be some character in *your* story—no mention of my bones which give me constant pain, something I live with like some people live with a hum in their ears or an unfaithful spouse. My body will disappear, yet here it sits, brittle in this rocker, hard wood scratching at my thighs through my pants' worn cloth. What I need's a soft cushiony La-Z-Boy built for a Miami landlord. But none of this gets written into your story, so who will I become?

Do you think he wondered?

I mean, his life in his stories—did it do something to him?

I guess I'm spending my feeling here talking this out and all. Spending good hard coin. Well, you can only hoard so much. Margaret and I aren't exactly bringing down the sheaves with our fortune. But here. Boy, I'm tired. Feel tied to this chair, a lump of lard softening in the room's heat. But the excitement I had the day I'd met him stayed with me through that dinner of ham and beans. I'd tried to tell Margaret about who this Hemingway fella was, spewing my food in my eagerness to explain what I'd guessed. Then, after the meal, I walked into the kitchen as Margaret washed, and I took her into my arms. Jesse! she snapped, afraid for the dishes. But I jabbed her tickle spot. Honey, she tittered.

We left them dishes for the bed.

Surprised us a bit, my going on like that, us aging into classic models, though obsolete might be what you'd call us today, long since resigned to childless living.

After, I'm lying there content and rolling that day in my head. That evening and many to follow. And what does it total in dollars or gallons?

It can't change.

It's happened.

He's dead and we sit here talking about him.

But enough. I'm tired, I tell you. Enough of this talk. This was it, I tell you, my one true story. **Q**

Things

After her husband's death, she gave everything away—food processor, hi-fi, microwave, even her green-striped Fieldcrest sheets and towels. Most of it went to her husband's children from a first marriage. The children—grown-ups now—had protested at first, but once they got into the swing of it, they even began demanding things: the good china, golf clubs, her five-speed Mixmaster. Herb's youngest daughter laid claim to a Mexican wool sweater that had belonged to Rachel's father. Rachel just waved one hand faintly and said, "Take it, take it all." She still bundled up bagfuls for the Salvation Army. The rest she dragged out to the curb one damp, chilly spring morning for the trash collectors to haul away. People might have thought she was coldhearted, or hadn't loved her husband. That wasn't it. Herb's things still had a life of their own, but he had no life anymore.

The house itself, nearly empty now, sutained her for a little while, the way a shell does its animal; then there were hot showers to be taken, and the lawn to be mowed, but no towels and no lawn mower. She realized with a shock that she would have to buy new possessions to replace the old. That was the kicker—she could get along without her husband, but not without his things.

So, grimly, she set out to buy the necessities all over again. She shopped at the local mall, staying away from downtown. Those downtown blocks—half the stores gutted and with soaped-up windows; the drunk who sang Irish tenor on the corner, the hard-faced teen-agers in skimpy T-shirts waiting for their buses in the cold—all made her feel like lying down in the street and crying.

The mall was different. It was a grown-up's Disney World, *Mister Rogers' Neighborhood* for adults, where after a while you got to know everyone on the block. There was Sears at the end of the street, and The Limited right next door to Friendly's, and JCPenney just around the corner. Other shoppers' faces swam toward her, then harmlessly away. It was always the same temperature, always the same hour and degree of daylight at the mall. Seasons came and went, and the only thing that changed was the greenery in tubs around the benches and fountains. You could walk for miles and never end up anyplace unexpected.

At first, she bought only one or two small things a day. Gradually, building up strength, she bought more, and learned to watch for sales, to wait for the final red-lined markdown. This required diligence and patience, an ever-vigilant eye. It wasn't that she needed bargains—shopping became a way of being, an occupation that extended itself indefinitely in ever-widening circles. If she saved five dollars off the Corning Ware pie plate, she could get the cunning cherry-pitter almost for free. As long as the bath towels were twenty percent off, she might as well buy the matching fingertip towels with rose-colored seashells appliquéd in satin.

But then she began to falter, to return a few things. Her self-confidence wavered. Herb had always been there, someone she could turn to and say, "Do you really like this color?" or "Which pattern do you like better—this or this?" Even if he was in another room, or barely glanced up from his book, it was easier making decisions with him there. If she made a mistake, they could live with it together. Now she had to bear the brunt of it, good or bad. She had no one to talk with, no one with whom to crow over a special bargain, a remarkable purchase. The brand-new thing kept you company only as long as it was hidden inside its stapled bag. As soon as you took it out, all its transforming magic drained away, and there you were, alone with something you had paid $17.95 for, plus tax.

It was her own fault. If she could only get it right, she felt, this moment of defeat would never happen. So instead of returning purchases for cash, she asked for store credit—which created still further trips to the mall, to find a way to use up the credit—but then she'd change her mind about those purchases, too, and it went on and on like that every day, including Sundays, till the daisies planted all around the mall gave way to a profusion of summer greenery, and the hill outside Montgomery Ward was banked with red snapdragons and pink petunias.

The saleswomen began to recognize her. A few even greeted her by name. She worried whenever she returned something—were they working on commission? and if so, would they lose it?—so she bought something more expensive the next time, to make up for it. The salespeople were always understanding. "The gray's much prettier anyway," they would tell her graciously, or, "You know, the trouble with polyester curtains is they don't wash up nice. You were right to exchange them." The older women made jokes about their aching feet while the young girls talked about their dates after work. "Not too long now," they'd tell her, lifting their small pretty wrists to peek at their watches. "Only a few minutes to go!" with a cheeriness that amazed her. She had come to dread closing time at nine o'clock.

It was the only bad time at the mall—those last twenty minutes before the stores shut down for the night. The metal gates at the front of the stores rattled halfway down, like something in a dungeon, and each interior noise took on a life of its own—the heavy drone of a vacuum cleaner, the clatter and wheeze of the cash register doing readouts for the night. Someone at the front of the store would turn off the Muzak and in the dead silence that followed you could practically go deaf. Suddenly she'd be the last one left in the store. The other shoppers—for there was safety in numbers—had drifted out gradually, leaving her alone and exposed. The salesgirls moved through the empty store like a small efficient army, hanging, folding, wheeling racks inside.

It was during these last few minutes that she would dart

into a new store, one that hadn't quite yet closed its doors, grab a blue tablecloth off the display table and throw the package onto the counter, as breathless as an Olympic runner, only to turn around while the salesgirl was ringing up her sale and see a prettier one in pink on a shelf right behind her, for six dollars less. But was pink too loud? Was navy too drab? One or two other customers would be pushing listlessly through the racks, making the lonely scraping sound of metal clothes hanger on metal pole. The pink tablecloth was a cotton/linen blend, which was pretty and soft, but the blue had a no-spill finish, and was more practical.

By the end of the evening, the salesgirls' faces were impassive masks, yielding nothing. Rachel could feel her own face grow pinched and drawn; sometimes she would groan out loud, her hands clenched into sweaty fists on the countertop. Whichever tablecloth she bought, she would no sooner walk out from under the fluorescent lights of the store than she'd *know* that she had made a terrible mistake; the thing would seem to die before her very eyes like a flower snatched out of water. There was always the chance to go back and return it the next day—the mall was open even on holidays—but she would have to live with it overnight, agonizing over her idiocy, her lack of decisiveness, trying to convince herself she had made the right choice. As soon as she got home, she'd set the dining room table with the new tablecloth, using her new flowered napkins, and when the pink cloth looked garish with these, she would take out the new Mikasa china, to see if it worked any better. This would occupy her right up to Johnny Carson, and then she'd have to grab her dinner during a commercial and go to bed without a shower. Sometimes she knew smack in the middle of paying for an item that it was all a mistake, just another mistake; she'd have to turn around and exchange it the next day. But what could she do? The saleswoman was already holding out her hand for the money. Rachel would drive home in the dark with her stomach muscles knotted up and the palms of her hands and soles of her feet stretched tight, her car flying over the State Street Bridge toward home.

After an evening like this, she'd come home only to find herself unnerved by every choice—should she park on this side of the street, or that side? under the maple tree, or out in the open? Should she have a tuna sandwich for dinner, or a bowl of soup, or both?

She would wrestle the last of her new purchases out of their bags, white tags dangling, just as the opening drum-roll music for *The Tonight Show* came on. Some nights the things would have to sit in their bags till morning. She never missed Johnny Carson, not even when he had guest hosts sitting in, but she liked it best when everyone was in his place—Johnny, and his sidekick, Ed McMahon, with his raucous and pained laughter—Haw! Haw! Haw!—and Doc Severinson the bandleader in his funny, glittery jackets. It was like having your own family reunited after a long absence, a real relief. By the time that was over, it was time for bed. On bad nights she might stay up and watch back-to-back reruns of the *Mary Tyler Moore Show*, or thumb through one of the magazines she subscribed to. She compared what she saw in those pages with what she had seen in the mall, and sometimes it made her reconsider what she'd bought, sent her scurrying back the next day to exchange one thing for another up-and-coming item ("Red is Hot This Year!") she'd nearly overlooked.

How did the other shoppers do it? She watched people buy entire households in the time it took her to select a metal colander. These were young women—undoubtedly single—pretty and impatient, who piled the things onto the counter as if they'd never had a second thought in their heads, nothing on earth to lose by a mistake. For Rachel, the more she bought, the less she could call her own. Her long happy life with Herb receded further and further into the past, buried under a mound of bath mats and dishtowels, throw pillows and polyester-filled comforters.

One evening, shortly after 9:00 PM, when Bradlees had just slid its glass doors shut behind her, she decided to sit down in the mall for a few minutes and catch her breath. The last of the late-night shoppers streamed past her, angling for the fastest way to the exits like balls in a pinball machine. She had just bought an outdoor gas grill that she was convinced she could never learn to use. The young man who'd sold it to her was restless, kept glancing over her shoulder as if she were a dull companion instead of a valued customer. "It's easy," he told her impatiently. "Read the directions. I'm sure your husband can figure it out." The box it came in was large, flat, and cumbersome, and because she'd bought it so close to nine o'clock she hadn't had the courage to ask anyone to carry it out to the car.

She sagged onto a slatted wood bench outside of Red Cross Shoes, leaned the cardboard box against her knees, and shut her eyes. For an instant she considered how it would feel to walk out into the cool summer's night air, leaving the grill behind her on the floor, and never come back to the mall again. Her heart opened up at the thought, then instantly clenched again. What on earth would she do with herself? She shifted the slippery box upward in her arms, to get a better grip. It was silly to throw money away. There were plenty of other things at Bradlees she could exchange it for. All she needed was a minute or two to gather her wits.

"Ma'am?" The man's deep voice blared like a voice on a car radio.

She opened her eyes.

A mall security guard was bending toward her. He wore a light blue cap and navy windbreaker; a huge keyring filled with keys dangled from his belt loop. He had a middle-aged paunch, and the paunch sagged toward her as he bent. "You sick?" he said.

"No," she said.

"Just nervous?"

"Nervous?" she said. "No, I'm—" He held out a large

hand to her and she took it automatically, pulling herself to her feet. The gas grill slid to the floor. "I'm fine, thank you," she said. "I was just catching my breath."

"Nobody's allowed here after hours." His pale blue eyes bored into hers. His mouth was unsympathetic.

"I'm sorry," she said.

He waved her words away. Then he reached out and lightly kicked the cardboard box with the tip of one shiny black shoe, leaving a scuff mark on it. "You need help with this?"

"No," she said curtly. She stood and hefted the big box, the cardboard slippery as a fish in her arms.

The security guard was standing with his hands on his hips, his eyes narrowed, as if he thought she might try to break into Red Cross Shoes and steal something. "I'll escort you out," he told her.

"That's not necessary," she said.

"It's my job." They walked side by side without saying a word till they'd reached the row of metal telephones just outside the double exit doors. "And don't let me catch you back here before tomorrow morning," the man said loudly. "Get some sleep!"

Rachel felt she'd been reprimanded like a child. Her face was flushed and stinging. She hoisted the Bradlees box a little higher in her arms, and though the guard held one of the glass doors open for her, she pushed her shoulder against the other door and stalked out without saying thank you or good night.

That whole next day she stayed away from the mall. She spent most of the morning trying to decode the instructions that had come with the outdoor gas grill. The manual was written in five languages, but she didn't understand any of them, least of all the English. Herb had kept a set of screwdrivers somewhere in the house, but she hadn't the faintest idea where, and resisted the impulse to drive to Sears and buy a new one. Instead she called a neighbor. The husband, a retired electrician, said he'd be delighted to help her put the grill together. He located Herb's toolbox in the garage, and

showed her how to use a Phillips screwdriver. He complimented her on her choice of grill. "This is a good one," he
said. "I wish I'd of bought the model with the heavy-duty cover
myself. You have the utensils to go with it?" He told her about
a store downtown that specialized in grills, barbecues, fire-
places, and cooking equipment. She wrote down the address
and thanked him for his help. "Invite us over for a barbecue
sometime," he said. "Now that the kids are all gone, Louella's
going crazy. Don't be such a stranger."

The next afternoon she went grocery shopping at the new
supercenter, and the day after that she stayed home and wrote
thank-you notes to all the people who had sent sympathy cards
months earlier. But on the fourth day it rained—there was a
feeling of fall chill already in the air—and she drove to the mall
because she'd seen the ads for the August white sales. She fell
back into her old patterns, taking care not to run into that
particular security guard again. When she spotted him lumber-
ing down the corridor, she crossed over to the other side of
the mall, or ducked inside a store till he had passed.

By September the mall was starting to fill up again, after
the relative emptiness of summer, first with the back-to-school
buyers, then with the early Christmas shoppers. Orange mums
replaced the summery greenery in the cement square around
the central fountain, and Halloween decorations dangled or-
ange-and-black skeletons in every store window. In the central
court, Elvis Presley's brother was selling copies of his autobi-
ography from inside a plywood booth. He was middle-aged,
with a heavy face and light brown hair slicked back Elvis style.
Over his head hung a neon sign, *Meet David Stanley, Elvis'
Stepbrother! Get Your Autographed Copy of "LIFE WITH ELVIS"!* People
were skirting the plywood booth as if it advertised a contagious
disease. Two teen-age girls in short skirts sat on a bench near
the booth, giggling, eating ice-cream cones, and calling questions to the man inside the booth.

"What was Elvis really like?" one of the girls shouted.

Elvis's stepbrother blushed. He had the kind of pale skin

that mottled easily, red and white. "He was a real nice guy," he said.

Rachel felt sorry for the man, and walked closer to his booth. She picked up a copy of the book and pretended to study the back cover with interest.

"How much is your book?" Rachel asked. She didn't really care; she intended to buy one.

"Sixteen ninety-five," the man snapped. "Plus tax."

She opened her pocketbook. "Will you take a check?"

"Sure." He looked embarrassed.

"It's a local check," she said. "And I have two forms of ID."

"Sure, sure," he said uncomfortably. "You want me to sign it for you?" He removed a ballpoint pen from his shirt pocket, and then hesitated, the hand holding the pen hovering over the flyleaf of the book. "Name?" he asked.

She felt even sorrier for him, and when he looked at her, she said gently, glancing up at the neon sign first, prompting him, "David Stanley."

He stared at her as if she were crazy. "I mean *your* name. Who do I sign it *to*?" he asked.

"To Herb," she said.

"Your husband, huh?"

She hesitated. "My husband is dead," she said.

She tore the check from her checkbook and slid it over the counter toward him. He waited till she met his eyes.

"Would you like to go get a cup of coffee?" he asked.

"I don't drink coffee," she said, hoping it would be that easy. But he had a dogged, stubborn look now.

"Well, what *do* you drink?" he asked. "Tea? Milk?"

She glanced left and right, as if looking for a visible escape hatch, when behind her came a loud, low voice, like something heard over a megaphone. "Taking a break?"

David Stanley looked flustered. "Yes, we—"

"I need fifteen minutes' notification if you're taking a break." The man who was speaking pushed past Rachel, and she recognized the security guard who had thrown her out of the mall. Her feeling of gratitude changed to anger.

"Can't this man have a cup of coffee?" she demanded.

"Not unless I have advance notice for one of my men." The security guard stared at her forehead, avoiding her eyes. She was sure he remembered her. She turned back to Elvis's stepbrother. "I'll be glad to bring you coffee," she said.

The security guard was openly sneering at them. His meaty hands were too big to fit into his pockets, so he put his thumb and pinky in, and let the other three fat fingers dangle awkwardly outside. He walked a few steps away, shoes clack-ing—close enough to keep an eye on them.

Rachel hurried to the Everything Yogurt stand and back again with a lidded Styrofoam cup of coffee. By now, she and David Stanley could barely look at each other. The security guard was standing in the same spot, his hands in a military at-ease position. He pretended to be studying the customers trickling in and out of JCPenney across the way.

"Thanks very much," David Stanley said, accepting the cup of coffee.

"It was nothing," she said. There was so much vehemence in her voice that the security guard, startled, forgot to pretend he wasn't listening. His head turned toward her for an instant, as if on a pivot, then quickly away again. He moved one hand nervously, and his fingertips grazed the holster of his gun.

"We're lucky he didn't shoot us," she said, loud enough for him to hear.

David Stanley was straightening his piles of books. Either he hadn't heard her, or he pretended not to. "Have a nice day," he said.

The security guard smiled.

The Halloween mall decorations were exchanged for turkeys and Pilgrim cutouts, and then overnight, it seemed, the Christmas displays came up. Center Court was trans-formed into a North Pole, with cotton snow and red poinsettias replacing the yellow and orange mums. You could hardly walk down the mall without bumping into some irate shopper. Scuffles broke out between strangers over parking spaces. The corridors were filled with loudly weeping children and enraged parents. Rachel overheard one little girl tell her mother, "I'm so happy Christmas is coming!" The woman barely glanced at her child. She dragged her along the mall as if the girl had no feet.

Every register had long lines, and the salespeople were temporaries. They didn't know or care anything about the merchandise. "Do you want it or don't you?" one teen-age girl snapped as Rachel stood debating over a countertop micro- wave. Everything was full price. A lot of common items were sold out completely. In one store, gloves and hats were dumped into bins, and from there shoppers spilled them onto the floor, rummaging around for the right size. One woman grabbed Rachel's own red leather glove out of her hand.

"That's my glove," Rachel said.

"I saw it first," the woman protested.

"You don't understand," Rachel said, producing the matching glove from her coat pocket. "It's my *glove.*" Even so, the woman was reluctant to give it back.

Rachel stumbled down the mall, driven from one store to the next by the force of the crowd. The same Christmas carols played over and over, and it felt as if all the air in the place were being sucked up into the loudspeakers.

She staggered over to a splashing fountain outside of Friendly's, and found a small clear space between two teen- aged boys drinking Fribbles. She sank down on the bench and buried her head in her hands, breathing hard. A few seconds later she heard what she thought was a chorus of angels. For the briefest instant she thought she had died and ascended directly out of the mall. Then she opened her eyes, and looked up. A local church choir had gathered next to the fountain, and was singing "O Come, All Ye Faithful." The elderly singers all wore red and white. The men wore red jackets, and the women wore floor-length red skirts with white blouses. They opened their mouths wide, like children, though most of them had white hair.

Shoppers pressed closer to hear the music. It was nine o'clock, closing time. The choir sang "Good King Wenceslas," "Jingle Bells," "We Wish You A Merry Christmas," and "Silent Night," and then dispersed to a smattering of applause from the last shoppers. Lights in the display windows blinked off, but the tinsel still hung in luminous garlands, shining in the darkness. Store managers glanced at her, locking up their front doors, then hurrying out into the cold.

It was quiet, windless, almost as if it might begin snowing right there in the mall. She went on sitting on the wooden bench, her elbows resting on her knees, one shopping bag at each foot. She felt peaceful, contented for the first time in months. If she shut her eyes, she could have slept right there in the empty corridor. Then she heard heavy footsteps treading down the hall toward her, and a jangling of keys.

She jumped up from the bench.

If she raced for the exit, she would have collided with the fat security guard. Instead she grabbed her bags and darted into the ladies' room next to Ups and Downs. The rest-room door swung softly behind her. The guard's heavy footsteps came closer. Rachel didn't dare turn on the light. She stood in the darkness, breathing quietly. The footsteps faded, and a large metal gate crashed closed nearby. The security guard whistled tunelessly, and headed back the other way, opening and closing another gate down the hall. She listened until she could no longer hear his whistling. Even so, she waited a few minutes more to be sure he was gone. Then she crept out into the corridor.

She was locked between two metal security gates, with two or three hundred yards between them, about ten stores' worth on either side. All the lights were off, except a few dim yellow security lamps, and the glow coming from a few stores where someone had left a light on in back. There was a curious sense of weightlessness, of lightness and peace in the corridor, the way she imagined life after death. The mannequins seemed to be dreaming of all the wonderful places they'd be going in their holiday velvets and taffetas, with their ski sweaters and ski poles. She strolled from one darkened store to the next, peering deep into every window the way a child gazes into people's houses at night. There was nothing to buy, and no one left to buy it from. She marched quietly up and down the corridor—staying away from the security lights at either end—till she knew by heart the price of every pump in the Buster Brown window, every flannel shirt in the BigMan TallMan clothing store. She crept a little further along, and looked at the sweaters in the Gap, and suddenly such a feeling of sadness and loneliness overcame her that she turned and glided back into the ladies' room. She washed her face at one of the sinks, dried her hands on a rough paper towel, then sat opposite the door with her coat wrapped around her. She drifted into sleep.

She jerked awake when the light snapped on, flooding the room. Once again she was staring at the tips of the security guard's shiny black shoes, the light blue pants with the dark stripes. She heard him give a loud shout, and saw one hand go to his gun. But then he recognized her, and flushed deep red, first with embarrassment, then with anger. "I don't believe what I'm seeing," he said.

Rachel stood up.

"Are you sick?" he asked.

She shook her head.

"Then what the hell are you doing?" he said. "A woman your age hanging around here—I get teen-agers all the time, trying to pull this kind of stunt. But these are teen-agers— teen-agers are confused!"

"I'm sorry," she said.

"Sorry has nothing to do with it!" he yelled. "A mall is not a place to live!"

She kept staring fixedly at his shiny black shoes, the droopy black laces hanging over the sides.

He sighed. "Lady," he said. "I don't want you hanging around here anymore. I'm calling your husband to come and get you."

"My husband is dead," she said.

The man pulled off his light blue cap. His hair was gray and rumpled-looking underneath, like a bed in which someone's been tossing and turning. "I'm sorry," he said.

She said, "Herb was an inventor over at IBM. He had a camera collection, and a beautiful rock collection. He could build anything. He kept pieces of bird's-eye maple and cherry heartwood around to work with. He made a little shop out over the garage. We kept a croquet set there, and in the summer evenings we would set it up on the lawn and play. He bought me anything I ever wanted. He even had a special set of gold clubs made in Scotland on our honeymoon." And by telling him about her husband's pruning shears, tool chest, fine silk jackets and ties, she at last came close to saying what it was she had lost. **Q**

The Men Are Here

Please come in. I think Mom is ready. Pop built the house for us.

This should not take long. Mom is in bed. My old room is upstairs. Mom says that she wants to stay in the house. This was Pop's easy chair.

Mom picks at her food. Would you like something to drink? We have asked for a private room. Pop drove the car. We have ordered TV. The neighborhood has changed.

We should turn down the heat. Mom has insurance. The minister stopped here. Pop always said to do what was right. I sign checks for her.

They tell us that this is the right thing for Mom. New people live next door. Mom has trouble walking. I run the car. We built a barbecue out back.

Mom has to sign some forms for us. We have to water the plants. Mom calls me at work. This house is too big. Do you believe in an afterlife?

We took care of Pop in the downstairs room. Mom looked better at Christmastime. They have visiting hours from four to eight. Pop and I were alone at the end.

Mom asks me to check the mail for her. Are your parents still alive? I saw Pop with tubes down in his throat. Mom gave me the keys.

Pop could not talk. I think I hear Mom. The doctor will see us today. We could close off the second floor. I did what Pop wanted me to.

Come on upstairs. Mom fell last month. You must be used to this. I held Pop's hand. We can carry her. Mom's old friends are gone.

Go on in. Say hello to Mom. Tell her you are here. **Q**

RICHARD BLANCHARD

Cleopatra

I think Cleo is coming into heat. My wife went up-stairs to rest.

Cleo hoists up her leg, and she noses and sniffs.

My wife does not feel well.

"Come over here, girl—let me take a look."

The boys are grown up and gone.

My wife keeps the house all spic and span. The hunting is good this year. We let Cleo come in through the kitchen door when it gets like this outside.

Cleo flops herself down by the kitchen stove. My wife has ups and downs. Cleo wags at me. I should clean the floor. The boys used to hunt with me.

My wife has these spells that come and go.

"Cleo, you're my sweetheart, girl."

You should see how Cleo works a field. I sleep in the boys' room now.

I am heating the broth up for my wife. Cleo says things to me with her eyes. I take my wife in to the doctor in town. Cleo rubs against my leg.

A man in town has this he-dog. My wife wears a sleep mask. Cleo is never allowed in the house except on the kitchen floor.

We moved the TV to my wife's room. This he-dog has papers too. The doctor explains that these woman things happen when a woman gets to this time of life.

I have seen Cleo push through the kitchen door. I miss the boys these days. Cleo sneaks up the stairs and comes into my room. The pills my wife takes do not work.

Cleo's coat feels smooth as silk to me. I think I hear my wife. In the night I wake up and touch Cleo, and she gets closer and touches me back.

I think that the broth is ready now.
"Cleo—you better stay here."
I have got to figure out what to say.
I will promise to do all the work.
"I will fix up a box for the puppies, girl."
I will promise to keep the door shut. **Q**

Teaching a Boy How to Climb

My boy is behind me. My father once brought me here. The trail is getting steep. We are making good time. The boy is quiet these days. I jog three times a week. My father has climbed the high peaks out West. These boots have nonslip soles.

The boy can drive the car next year. We brought crampons just in case. Our tent is pitched down at the trail head. I wish Pop could see the boy.

My father always set the pace. The boy has the water jug. My knee hurts. The boy could have gone with his friends. My cholesterol is down.

My father would never stop to rest. I am teaching the boy to climb. It is getting warm. You have to pick your spots. People say the boy looks like me.

We are climbing the same trail my father took. I bought the boy new boots. The sweat is getting in my eyes. He is my only son.

I say one foot and then the other. I am talking to myself. The fuzz on his chin is turning dark. My father was slowing down.

The boy is as tall as I am now. I heard my father breathing hard. The boy does not ask me for help these days. I am climbing as fast as I can.

We are up on the steepest part of the climb. My father said to breathe through the mouth. I see where we are. It happened here. I can hear the boy behind.

I passed my father here.

I see the top.

It is not too far to go. **Q**

Erection Stress

François reads the copy of *The Chronicle* he has borrowed from Tom Pace. "We now have an environment that is difficult to work in," says the President of the United States.

> So you separate yourself from your environment. You don't watch what you eat, what you walk into. You stop looking out for abandoned cars, or suspicious old men in front of Muslim hospitals. And the moment you stop being cautious, you start to disintegrate.

By the time François meets the nurse at the Obeids' party, he is already half gone. He can already see between the carpals in his hand, as it grasps the edge of the table. He has to anchor himself: otherwise, he will be blown away by her words.

"How did you get . . . ?" Her scrubbed hand traces the marks from face to throat.

> Sometimes, you just get tired. You get tired of being careful. You get reckless again, like a child running, dodging potholes. You have accidents.

The Riyadh weather report said hot and dry. It is Thursday, the day before the Sabbath, and François has the day off. On Thursdays, he usually stays in his room in the Old City, reading the newspapers. The room has thick mud walls, a desert cooler, and a carved wooden door. It is quiet and dim and, directly outside, there is a variety of peace.

The third prayer call of the day begins. It echoes from the roadside mosque across the new six-lane highway. It climbs over the steady throb of the desert cooler.

"You know, of course, that it is only a recording," says François. He sits beside her on the bed, moves the pages of the *Herald Tribune*.

"No," she says. "I didn't."

"There was a contest," he says, untying her black head scarf. Her hair is bleached, the color of lemons. He touches her breasts, under the dark tunic. She was wearing the tunic—good girl—like an Egyptian, when he stopped the car at the hospital dormitory. She got in the back as if he were her driver—good.

"The best mullah was chosen," he says. "Now you hear the same voice everywhere in the city, at simultaneous intervals. It is all synchronized by computers—a joint development project between this country and yours. God is Great."

"I wish you hadn't told me."

"I'm sorry."

The nurse sips her drink, paces off his room. He sees her feet sink into his tile floor, leaving large sharp prints. "You can pray if you want," she says, looking toward Mecca, then to the floor.

You try to keep things light, just make conversation.
But it doesn't work. They can see your history, the
pink scars snake under your collar, and all they can
hear are symbols. They hear Sorrow and Fate and
Resignation.

"Thanks, but I only pray with my uncle," he says. "When I get leave."

Every six months François gets leave. It is part of his benefits package with the Airport Expansion Project, which is run by Californians. The Californians provide him a round-trip ticket, but only as far as Jiddah, the Red Sea, because Beirut is not a recommended vacation spot. So François will go on from Jiddah, under his own recognizance.

François is glad he is with the Airport Expansion Project. He is learning a great deal about American engineering. He strokes her body, sees brushed aluminum, gold-tipped warheads. She is firm and sleek—and almost hairless—like the Thai children the American men talk about. The Americans go

East for their vacations: to Bangkok, Singapore, San Francisco.

The nurse is going East. She and her roommate will visit Sri Lanka. But not, of course, on an authorized tour. They will go on their own recognizance.

"There are fewer places every year," she says, "where one can safely go." She stretches under his thin sheets, and the narrow bed creaks under her weight. "The travel agent: 'Ah, Beirut—the Paris of the Middle East. It's too bad.' "

"There was a time, a window," says François, "when you could have gone. You could sun all morning by the Mediterranean, then ski in the mountains the same afternoon."

"But now is not the time, the agent said. Everyone who is anyone has already left."

The Obeids have left. They are now Lebanese-Americans; they give mixed parties. The Obeids have done well in the kingdom: they have American passports and a home in Virginia. They speak all three languages.

"I love to hear you speak," says the nurse, kissing him firmly. "The way you mix everything up." He speaks to her mostly in French, because she does not understand French.

"Take *ennui,* for instance." He holds his drink, stands close to her as Mrs. Obeid explains. "There is no English word. No French for *Inshallah,* no Arabic for *computer.* " He sees she is rapt, entirely attentive to the words. There is no part of her that is held in reserve, watching over her shoulder, listening for midnight knocks.

His elbow almost touching, he feels how solid, how substantial she is. Within her body is the weight of infrastructure—massive marble banks, bunkers of aimed missiles, whole armies of agencies. Her wide clear eyes reflect a lifetime of peace under cold still skies—an idyll of unarrested sleep, of drive-in movies and coitus uninterrupted.

She is from Atlanta but can travel anywhere. At this particular time, she tells him, there is a definite care shortage. "So I could work anyplace, really." In the kingdom, she says, she is learning a great deal. She is meeting people of varied cultural backgrounds, witnessing glaucoma and tuberculosis and other nomadic diseases.

And she has always been adventurous, even back home. "So what?" she said, when she had first come to the room. "What's the worst that can happen if we are caught? Flogging?"

"I just want you to be aware of the law," he told her. "If we are caught"—he sees uniforms at the door, embarrassed shufflings, rifles—"you may in fact be deported."

Deportation. Remember, this was one of the first English words you learned. The word, like other English words—like bunker, like bomb—came from a time long ago when wars were distinct and numbered. A war, Baba said, had a beginning and an end. Now we have no more wars, Baba said. We have disturbances, clashes, coups. But, although there are no more wars, we still need the words of war. Zones of occupation. Shrapnel.

"I refuse to be deported," she says. "I'll just go somewhere else." She has already camped in the desert, attended a Saudi wedding, eaten goat meat with the cultural attaché.

"But what would happen to you?" she says. The weight of her hand settles on his chest, passes through it, falls on the sheet under him. He doesn't breathe.

You just get so tired of being careful, crossing and recrossing the streets, watching, listening in the night. You want to play with any child you choose.

He will go to jail. "For how long?" she asks.

"Not long," he says. "But—I will lose my work permit."

A prince, not just a prince but a brother of the king, fourteenth in line, is building a new palace. A section of the Old City has been demolished to make room. If the Californians agree to build the palace, then the prince will help clear the Bedouins from Landing Strip #12.

Tomorrow, François and Tom Pace will meet with the royal contractor. They will go to the site where François will translate HRH's building requirements. François is flattered that Tom Pace has asked him.

Tom Pace has spoken to François before. Would he like to live in L.A.? Go to graduate school? These things have been spoken of casually, over beer and a televised soccer game.

As they stumble over rubble—the Lebanese, the Saudi, and the American—François will try not to think about California. He will try not to think about leaving Lebanon forever, about raking leaves, riding the freeway, buying a car and a swing set. Beside him, the Saudi points out a movie theater, a sports complex, separate housing for guests, servants, women.

"I would like to go somewhere else," François tells the nurse. Or else he would like to lie here his whole life, reading the newspapers. He reads all the newspapers—*Le Monde, The New York Times, The Saudi Gazette*—trying to understand what has always been happening to him. He reads the words from the outside, where people have perspective.

"The problem is that the need to have dialogue is no less important than before," says *Le Monde*.

The problem is that you cannot lie still or go. You have important work here; you get paid. Here you are part of progress. At home you are just part of the problem.

This is progress: the people are rolling in excited off the dry deserts, oblivious of the careful construction quotas of the Five-Year Plan, the Fifteen-Year Plan. They believe they have been invited to an extravagant worldwide feast. No one knows when the feast will begin, but no one wants to be left out. So they drive their bleating goats onto the vacant land near the old airport, next to crumbling palace walls. They anchor their black wool tents to Citibank. There is a definite shortage of infrastructure.

The Old City is being overtaken, a joint economic project planned by Americans, Saudis, and Japanese. Grids are drawn, walls are blasted. Every day the blasts come closer and closer to François's door, and he cannot sleep.

You sit up straight in the bed. Your father is calling from the courtyard outside your room. "Enough," says Baba. "I'm coming." Then you hear what woke you, the steady unhurried banging of a fist on the street door. You creep out into the cool yard. "Go back to bed." From the shadow of the olive trees, Uncle whispers, scolding. But from the light of Baba's lamp, you see out into the street. You see rows of dark green sweat pants, tennis shoes. You see a rifle held slackly by its strap. You see your father go out into the street, in his pajamas. He turns, and pulls the iron door shut.

François goes from door to door, negotiating for landing strips. Sometimes, there are no doors. Whenever a high wind spins off the desert, he must stop and hold tight to a tent rope, tethering himself to the sand. Then the Bedou come in droves, cluck their tongues at François's situation. But they pity him and often invite him in, to drink tea and pray and watch the eight o'clock news. "Fifty thousand explosions in a single night," says the woman grasping the microphone. She stands on a hill outside Beirut. A rough wind brings tears to her blue eyes.

By the time she is in his bed, he is almost weightless. She closes her hand around his vanishing wrist, unconsciously checking his pulse. He sees her move her middle finger, try again to locate a heartbeat. The sheer mass of her curiosity is the only thing that holds him to the bed.

"How did you get . . . ?" Her hand traces the marks from face to hip. He feels her looking at his past, trying it on.

"I went out," he shrugs, embarrassed. He is not used to women staring. "I went to a movie."

"Oh."

"I was supposed to meet someone—after." He almost has it, the name of the movie. Which Bond was it—Connery or Moore? He cannot see the face but he hears the voice. "Stirred, not shaken."

"What?"

"Maalesh, Habeebti." Nothing, my dear. Just.

"Yes." She moves her hand down, traces the ragged circumcision that has exposed him since birth. He lies passive under her, playing hostage.

Ali, the prison guard, will smuggle in a copy of the *Herald Tribune.* "If mutual deterrence does not work," says the former secretary of defense, "the only recourse is suicide."

But you were still mortal then. So you hesitated right outside Uncle's courtyard door, sniffing the air. The air was clear, undusty; and the wind was from the sea. You walked down the middle of the street, dodging potholes, past the place where Cedars Café used to be. Four green metal chairs still sat, unsalvaged, around a bare table. Two teen-age girls with veiled heads picked through rubble on the other side, near the place where the sidewalk dropped off last week. When they saw you watching, they giggled behind their hands and limped away, their long ragged skirts bright on the broken pavement. Except for the human remnants—the colored plastic bits, the shreds of cloth amid the blasted buildings—you could imagine the street was under construction, part of some vast urban renewal project.

You paused, again, at the corner, across from the hospital. That was when you decided to die—to take your life between your own hands. The street was too normal. Any child could tell. A city bus passed, belching black smoke. Two jeeploads of khaki soldiers sped through the intersection, just missing an old robed man. Women picked through oranges at a fruit stall near the burned abandoned car.

Outside a machine gun rapid-fires; he feels himself shrink inside her. "For Christ's sake, it's only rivets," she says. "Only construction."

"You can't do this," says God. "After all I've done for you, all my carefully wrought plans." So you do not die. But you do not live.

And you wish He would leave you the hell alone. You wish He would quit picking at lice, just step back and look at The Big Picture. Then you wish He would finally make up His mind and then send the flood, the bluest Sea rising up and drowning, selectively, one suburb and passing over another. Spare Fayadrize, slaughter Byblos, catch the Party of God in their beds: just do something! You wish He would get it over with once and for all—so people could sleep.

Later, she has turned away from him and faces the wall. He has a bad taste in his mouth, like coated metal. He can see he has disappointed her. He can see it in the way she reaches out and crushes a section of his wall in her fist, sifting the rockdust through her fingers. She sits up and plants her feet on the floor, blocking the air from the desert cooler.

She does not trust the desert cooler. "This is so stupid," she tells him, "to hook electric power to a box of wet straw."

"I suppose it is," he laughs, irritated. "But it works."

And you know what she is thinking. That the wounds should stand for something, yes. You should have been *doing* something, something constructive, at the time. How do you see me there? you want to ask. Saving children? Yes, that is how she wants to see you, the nurse. To picture you pulling babies from cement scrapple.

And you could kill her for that but you know you can't. Because she has all those years of sleep behind her and will just roll over you and crush you the minute you make a move. You caress the strong steel sinews of her throat and you know there is no way you could ever.

"You have to be careful what you get shot for," François tells her.

"Like a movie?" she says.

"Yes. To go to a movie—that's worth getting shot for."

"I feel like I've been dancing on a grave."

"I'm sorry."

He is dressed, but she is not, when the knocking starts on the carved wood door, over the whine of the desert cooler. He curses, wondering who has been watching his room, and for how long. "Enough," he says, getting up. "I'm coming." Then he laughs, giddy, as his feet rise. He hovers a meter above the floor.

"*I* got you out," says God. "*I* arranged California. And now you just throw it all away, on this, on this— girl."

He reaches for her Egypt clothes. But the black cloth slips through what is left of his flesh. The veil drops to the tile. She finally gets it, annoyed. The tunic tears as she forces her arms into the sleeves. "Goddamnit, what next?" She bangs the door open, thrusts out her passport as François floats, clutching the sill. Two uniforms, embarrassed shufflings. Subdued greetings all around.

The uniforms are not happy with this task. They remember Chicago, the special police training program at Northwestern. They were not properly trained for this. We have no choice, brother. You understand.

But they check the passports, determine François is not her husband, not her brother. But they already know, or they would not be at the door.

They go through the door into the desert: the nurse first, then François (drifting), then the police. All around them, there is suspended activity, halted destruction, as the workers stand, curious, rivet guns and piledrivers dangling from their hands. A thin veil of rockdust hangs in the air from yesterday's blast, obscuring the sun. François blinks in the bright heat, sees gray tanks, twisted car frames, desiccating limbs in rubble.

The nurse coughs drily as they walk through the ruins. "There was a restaurant." He looks at her, ignoring the police. "Right across the street—wasn't there?" But she does not answer, her face shadowed in black.

The policemen are arguing. They are arguing about where they will all sit in the police car. The woman rides alone, says one—in the back. The man can't ride in the front, he's under arrest, says the other. "Why don't you take my car?" says François. "I have the keys—here." "Thank you," say the two men. They are happy with his solution.

The new highway is not open to the public—it is empty and still. As they step onto the strip, the nurse's hard heels sink into the black asphalt, making sucking sounds. The wind kicks up suddenly, and she clutches at her skirt.

"Dust devil," Baba said, tickling you under the chin. "Don't look at it, Habeebi, or you will be swept away." But you watched anyway, from the street door, as it swept in from the desert and whirled through the neighborhood. It picked up everything in its path, grew fat with rubbish and large mammals. You watched it twirl, go clockwise, and then halt by your door, drop its load of carrion, and go whirling off in the opposite direction.

"Hezbollah Postpones Executions," said *The Saudi Gazette.* "That is a very pleasant surprise," said the President of the United States.

And you just let go.

"François," she calls. But by then you are already caught and swirling three meters, four, off the black road, out of the scope of her capable hands.

You can see her reaching up to you: her round open mouth, her trunk, her feet planted firmly on the asphalt, her truncated arms imploring you, like a child wanting her kite.

But now you have perspective. You see her take off from the New Expanded Airport with the cultural attaché.

You are already high above the road and could not come back. Even if you wanted to. You revolve slowly, looking out past the city over the desert, where the highway snakes off across the sand toward Mecca.

You see Los Angeles, City of Angels, hectares of parking lots, two-piece bathing suits.

You see buried teen-age girls rise from the ruins, their bright hair like lemons.

You see your father's courtyard door.

You see thirty thousand Syrian shells hit the entrance to a crowded Christian bomb shelter.

You see Maryland, Camp David. You see the Joint Emergency Evacuation Team deposit forty-six key personnel at the entrance to Raven Rock bunker.

You see the people marching in, off the deserts, out of starships. You see soldiers lining the sides of Airport Road, saluting diplomats from Uganda, Peking, and Washington.

You see two seas, from the West and from the East, meet and flood the road, the people swallowed up by a red tide.

The two graduates from Northwestern University shout, blow their whistles, plead. They will lose their jobs; they will never get back to Chicago. You see them take the straps from their shoulders and point their rifles into the wind.

The last thing you see is the woman again, poised over François this time: her sound calcium-rich bones, her flat strong stomach. And you remember how she could talk about anything—abortions, cancer, religion, Vietnam—while nibbling at the Obeid's oily buffet. She could eat anything. She talked of scrapple, a greasecake of sugar and pigs' snouts. She said it was one of her most vivid childhood memories. She said she wanted to take you, right there, in front of everyone.

She rides on you, hard, saying "Scrapple."

A hard German word.

Like ripping fabric. **Q**

Unable to Sleep, the Father
Fills Page after Page

My dear son. Your father again, bursting with queries. You will remember Mrs. Mackson, Irene Mackson, I am certain, if only for her hopeless opposition to your association with her daughter, the seduction of each of you by the other, and I should begin by telling you that her recent death and yet more recent funeral service (this afternoon) are the immediate causes of this effusion. There are, as usual, other causes, other agitations, no less fundamental. Certain cares are never put by.

Mrs. Mackson stood in this house only once. You were fifteen I believe, and Mrs. Mackson arrived to protest your attentions to young Karen Mackson's breasts. Even now I laugh to recall the scene. Poor Mrs. Mackson! Large with indignation, she called your crimes to our notice. What manner of boy, she wished to inquire, was growing wild within our walls. Were we aware of the problem? Oh, she was deeply embarrassed. "My daughter has told me . . . ," she sputtered.

What part of her anger was titillation, I wondered. I am sure her imagination was vivid. Every detail had been pried from her daughter, what you did and did not try. No little envy there, I suspected.

"So what is the matter?" I said, when she subsided. "You would prefer my Malcolm did not notice? You would prefer for this event to go unnoticed, this momentous but as yet unspectacular change? It is of no importance?" I smiled for her. I have known her from a child. We are both to be found, beaming and sullen, she and I, in a creased picture of the Roosevelt School third grade, class of 1927.

"Ralph," your mother said, "do not make jokes. Irene is upset." She too was smiling. The air soon cooled. Irene Mackson was persuaded to stay. She agreed to sit, and soon began to speak of old times. Happiness rose up in her eyes. Many things were remembered, our lives were brought out and polished in the air between us. Our tones grew soft. Our accents were those of care. Randy Gordon in particular was discussed—set-shot whiz, trumpeter, youthful love of Irene Mackson. Surely, I thought, it was Randy Gordon who took first notice, all grace and steadiness gone from his hands, of Irene Mackson's new and wonderful breasts. Then new and wonderful, though soon fallen. Refreshments arrived, were consumed and complimented. Our adventures lasted late into the day.

But now she is gone, dead, as Randy Gordon two years ago, fallen with unanticipated suddenness after thirty years' ascent in auto parts.

Incidentally, it may interest you to learn that your old love Karen Mackson returned to Scranton for her mother's funeral in the company of a young gentleman introduced as her intended. His name escapes me, but you will be relieved to hear that her husband-to-be is by no means so handsome as you, nor is he so young, if my guess is accurate. What he is, evidently, is rich. Nuptials are scheduled for the summer, and Karen Mackson made a point of hoping, so she said, that you would be in town. I think this would not be a wise thing. But death and matrimony—somehow their juxtaposition did not seem inappropriate, or without its solaces.

My life has reached the point where I meet with my contemporaries, my once-intimate friends, most frequently at funerals. How rapidly we sped off from one another, into our lives! I remember no intermediate time—we were together daily and then suddenly years, even decades, intervened between our meetings.

So now we have reached the point where our children are our confidants? Am I alone in this, or do you sometimes hear from your friends of similar parental initiatives? And it occurs to me too, when I move to the telephone or to my desk, in the evenings usually, with a strong urge upon me to speak with you, my son, and this urge comes with a frequency that might surprise you, it occurs to me to suspect myself for a windy bore, today's Polonius, so that often I am overcome by diffidence, and return to my chair.

But Laertes was burdened with advice, not questions, if I remember rightly. Is it, then, a mark of our age, a sign of our confusion, that we pass between our generations not credos, but attitudes of perplexity, postures for bewilderment?

I want you to know that I have appreciated, and have read with all my attention, the volume by Mr. James Agee, *Let Us Now Praise Famous Men,* sent to me by you some months ago. I remember also the fine and intense discussion of this book which occurred between you and your friend John, the one from Texas, I believe, during my last visit. We were on the subway, if you recall, on our way to dinner at a Chinese restaurant greatly favored by your circle of friends. I was permitted to pay, and I was happy to do so, for I must tell you I was astonished by all that happened. Your friends are so varied in their backgrounds, have gathered at the university from such scattered spots on the map, that they have seemed to me a marvelous and exotic band. Such vigor and confidence is new in my experience. Like a healthy band of pirates—this is how you seemed to me, rolling down the sidewalks of Chicago like a wave.

Can you have any sense of how closed, how very Balkan my own world was, by comparison? No hint of this continental scope which spins like a breeze from your friends. Your mother and I were born in the same town, acquainted long before high school. I had no friends in Texas, or from Georgia. Europe was less strange. Europe was in fact well represented in Scranton. I was scolded in many languages, by mothers of my friends.

For much of this difference credit is due to you alone. I remember it well. "I think I'll go to Chicago," you said. It was a good choice, it seems, a westering choice, in harmony with the choices of your forebears. Since then, I've tried to see that place, what it must be for you. Through visits and your letters, and of course through books. My own introductions were Studs Lonigan, Augie March. Nelson Algren and Studs Terkel were presents from you.

But in Mr. Agee's book, I was especially struck by the "Country Letter," near the beginning, where the author sits awake at night, the tenant family asleep around him, touched by the isolation of families, drawn together in fragile homes, enduring what I remember are described as the "assaults" of the universe. No doubt I am drawn to this passage, with its meditations on immemorial fluxings, ebbs and flows of generations, by my own disquiets, now centered on Irene Mackson.

But I was discussing your friends, comparing them with mine, and remembering the Chinese dinner. Do you recall what followed? Billiards! At a decidedly blue-collar parlor located above a taproom. Another ride on the subway was necessary. We entered by a narrow stairway, dimly lighted, and traversed by me with apprehension. Surely the building codes of Chicago address themselves to these matters. Bribes, of course, would explain everything.

I must tell you I was surprised that the ladies were admitted, in fact I recall the whole evening as a series of such surprises. I remember vividly your friend from Wisconsin, the burly fellow who met us at the billiard hall. His name was Jim, I believe. He had all the necessary gestures, didn't he? Had mastered that environment. I was impressed.

The young ladies, too, who have appeared in your company at our door, and who always seem to be vaguely in residence at your address during our visits—I must say that they are a stunningly attractive lot. Never have I known their like, these skittish thoroughbreds of yours from faraway places. I remember your letter from Connecticut last summer, during your visit to the home(s) of one of these. Of particular vividness is your account of the summer house in New Hampshire, on Lake Winnipesaukee (I have the *Goode's Atlas* in front of me) where the young lady's father answered your query as to the necessity for two airplanes by saying that one was for his short business trips, the other for his longer business trips. He left the next day for Saskatchewan.

Each new woman stuns and amazes me. Do you appreciate at all how lovely they are? I am sure they must be very hot numbers, and I worry only because they seem to share, be they from Phoenix or from Vicksburg, a generalized and abstracted anxiety unfamiliar to me. The roots of our anxieties—I speak for my whole generation, unblushingly—were usually all too obvious, all too present.

At first I wondered how you would fare in such speedy company. You were just eighteen, and it was clear to me from the start your ladies were slumming. Plumbing supplies, uncle's movie palaces, Polish and German spoken in the home—these were the topics which interested your guests. They were charmed.

Visions of Ellis Island were in their minds. Dark men of short stature. "My father can't even change a tire," said one, after wondering aloud concerning my abilities with a plunger. This only seemed to be a complaint. She was in fact bragging. "Someone will do it for him," I said.

I was tempted, in those days, to give you the dope on these babes, provide you with some fatherly advice. You understand I did not want that you should be in over your head with these people. Over my dead body you should be made a fool, run through the cleaners by some slender aristocrat whose Daddy flies off his lake to Saskatchewan.

Soon, however, I was at ease. Such fears were unfounded. He'll be all right, I told your mother. Better she should warn the girls. You gave them what they wanted, didn't you? For this you suddenly become Mike, instead of Malcolm? Your background turned to legend. Mike the hard rock. Old country ethnicity, am I right? I can imagine what an asset this is, in your designs. No effete blueblood is here, sheathed in a blazer and sucking a pipe. Nothing but muscle and lust.

I fill with admiration, and with pride. My son is no sucker. Much later, when this subject is discussed between us, we laugh together at your story of the father from Boston who opposed your coed travel plans, offered his girl an air ticket, which if accepted would stick you in Boston with a 1,000 mile solo drive back to Chicago. All this with you at his table, eating his eggs and toast—but you did not protest, had no need to protest. You knew he plotted in vain. I did feel some pain for the father. There are worse crimes than pomposity. His girl wanted blood, and you helped her.

But they are indeed lovely, these exotic ladies of yours, as strange and wonderful to me as your friends. It is difficult not to envy your frolics with such companions, but I am afraid I would not welcome your task should you ever undertake to live at length with one of them.

Of love itself I am certain we must have widely divergent views. With us (again I suppose my experience typical, of my time and of my place) I think love came late. Looking back, we saw that we had come to love. I think it grew unnoticed from appreciation.

Of course I found your mother beautiful—but my remembered moments of her loveliness are few. Most vivid is her face in the lights of a movie marquee—we are standing in line to purchase tickets. A light snow is falling, and large flakes sparkle in her dark hair. I am in uniform, soon to see the Pacific. I remember we were very happy. She told me I was handsome.

For you, I gather love has much to do with astonishment, is immediate and present. One perceives a woman, is dazzled by her loveliness, entranced by her proud bearing, her brilliant conversation—and is in love. For such a view there is of course the authority of great literature. The extreme case of Dante is well known.

My own recollections give me ladies wiping counters at F.W. Woolworth, or standing behind lunchroom cash registers. My adventures lacked the glamour of yours, I am sorry to say. Without entering into details, let me tell you I have strong memories of cabbage smells, and laundry soap. These were the musks of my first loves, older women who approached me boldly, without hint of romance. My hair was not tousled, as I remember yours was, throughout a long evening's conversation. My hand was not taken, except to be placed directly upon a breast of huge dimension, by way of invitation from a woman of perhaps forty whose groceries I had just delivered. I was sixteen. Your water bed, and vials of vaguely oriental body oils whose uses I can barely imagine—these hints of seraglio were not mine to enjoy. The whores of Scranton once relieved young men for the sum of five dollars, but in my single experience of this kind my partner refused to remove her brassiere.

When romance did arrive, finally, in my last year of high school, its initial climax occurred in the vestibule of the lady's home, a place for the storage of coats, with the aid of the lady's hand. Her father sat within, listening to the radio. We stood together, kissing and clutching, thrilled and terrified, both in our galoshes.

Love was a distant and exotic thing. I spoke of it often, knowing nothing, knowing only that girls were anxious to hear the word, were vulnerable to it as to a talisman or incantation. The best were brave and strong, expected little even in their youth, and were kind anyway. In time I came to appreciate these qualities. Finally, looking back, I realized that this was love, for me. Your mother was before this time wearing lop-sided pink slippers with dirty fur balls on their toes. Pipes and traps were strewn about her kitchen. You were nearly five, jealous and protective of your sisters, and I was back from Iwo Jima, fighting now for money. I began to think more about your mother, about her life. Her doings and endurings became for me occasions of wonder.

I have stopped, since the last paragraph, and gone to the refrigerator. It is after three o'clock. I have walked through all the rooms, turning on lights. Your mother was up for a moment. We had a cup of tea before she returned to bed.

How is it possible, that we make such attempts? Each one is locked away. No full recovery is available, no complete transcript. Who would persevere in saying even such a thing as a home, or a city block and its echoes? Who would have patience to listen? Wives and husbands. Sons and fathers. These more than others.

The effort is reciprocal. In such terms do I understand the many books which arrive with your highest recommendation. Also the bringing of your friends. So it is that I am up the night, seeking you, who are to me a nearly mythological creature, instead of Morgan, my friend since we were six. Believe me when I tell you it's new ground I cover in your company.

It is not always easy. You with your Jerry Lee Lewis, for example, and the herd of ancient black men with injured guitars. Before this, the strange Mr. Cocker, whose sufferings in a very popular moving picture we saw together several years ago could only be an occasion for pity and grief. But my own favorites, I know, fare no better in your ears.

In other areas, too, in the matter of living arrangements for example, we could not differ more. You were gone at eighteen, to live in various derelict rooming houses and rat-infested apartments with your friends. My recollection is clear, of the snap of activated mousetraps, throughout one evening of animated talk. This situation has made for friendships of great intimacy. The range is deep, but narrow. All who live at your addresses are your age.

Compare your father's youthful years. I lived at home until the Army intervened. Only the family was there—but Papa Schleuter was eighty-six, only fifteen years in this country. Papa sent for him when Grandmother died. He spoke no English, except to hammer on the wall and shout "coal" when his room grew cold at night. You do not remember him, though he lived to see you. "Fine," he said, in English also, when you were brought in to him.

Sister Margaret was there also, your aunt, with Walter, her new husband. A child soon came, your cousin Herschel, now selling insurance, a father himself. Under one roof—the whole trouble. Father making money, urging education upon me, upon Margaret, upon even poor Walter, so gentle and slow-witted. But most upon himself. He took correspondence courses—in accounting, in electrical appliance repair. The covers of matchbooks were filled out and mailed. Once he tried to sign up as an umpire of basketball games. This at fifty-nine, though of the game and its rules he knew nothing, because a buyer told him they were paid two dollars for each game. Have you heard these things, these old adventures of your blood?

Scope and depth—these seem again to name our separate ways. So it is I hear with admiration your discussion of the world's cities, your great experience of restaurants and museums. There was especially that fellow Zachary, whose reasons for rating the Prado collections, in Madrid, above all others were heard by me with high interest. Also your friend John, who told us during a visit of his summer in Vicenza, with particular enthusiasm for the structures of Palladio. This was recalled by me last summer, when I visited Mount Vernon with your mother, and heard a tour guide mention a Palladian window. Your mother was very impressed with my knowledge, and I am not ashamed to tell you I was happy. Tom Sawyer walks atop the fence for Becky Thatcher's applause. He does this all his life.

So it is that we persist, or so I understand our persistence. A large gulf yawns between us, between our generations, between our friends and loves. Effort is called for.

For questions of motive I have two answers. One is from a book and the other is from my own thinking. From my own thinking I see that you live in a far world, but with many of my wits. I do not deny my happiness in this. I think you have never called me a fool, and this I understand is not so very common. Many times I hear of daughters and sons saying in the faces of their parents harsh evaluations, as if they were guilty of horrible crimes, sins resulting in permanent trauma, scars on the little psyche and such. You have spared me this melodrama. So this is my first answer. In different worlds we have much in common. We often achieve intimacy, even across our years. Our wrath and laughter is close at the source. We share many glances. "I feel that way, too," they say.

My second answer comes from a book which may be unknown to you. *Psychoanalysis and Feminism,* written not long ago by a woman named Juliet Mitchell, is in fact a spirited defense of Sigmund Freud. Evidently he has his modern detractors, and these are effectively pulverized. But my interest was in Freud himself, who was quite a topic of up-to-date conversation among my night school friends. In Mitchell's volume I found one passage of extreme beauty. It took my breath away. The discussion concerns the origins of the infant's sense of himself or herself, and it is suggested that this momentous step is accomplished in an act of imagination. Here is a central sentence: "The helpless human baby, fascinated by the complete human faces and forms that he encounters, imagines his own future, and thus enters into a primary identification with the human form."

Does this also strike you? The author goes on to stress the necessary alienation in this process—the self is modeled on another. The infant looks at another and sees himself, herself, for the first time. It is a mistake. It is not himself. It is another. But from that moment a self, conceived and born in error, begins to walk its own path, begins to come true.

My own musings take a somewhat different direction. A parental perspective, it may be, but more exhilarating. How close the generations come, in this moment! The mother, and the father—they also are born again, into a new world. The infant gazes into the faces hovering above its cradle. Gazes again and again, and finally, in an act which must be love, appropriates that face, those faces made one, embraces them so desperately and completely that they are seized utterly, internalized. This is me, says that act. I am that. And the hovering faces, if they knew, would gaze at themselves as if into a mirror, would see themselves rising in the infant's features, would sense some essence transferred. This is other than genes and chromosomes. It is giving and taking. It is a meshing, an embrace. We are one, more deeply than we know.

Was all of this in Papa Schleuter's word to you, the "fine" he spoke before he died? Was this his last true word? I think again of Irene Mackson. Of Karen Mackson. Of you and me.

I hear the birds. Your mother will soon be up. I will make her breakfast. I will leave this space for her to write a note. For all of this, I claim a father's privilege.

It comes with love. **Q**

The New Century

Miller Logan was a man with horses. The horses came from the best stock in England, Persian and Arabian blood, their asses tight and muscular, their faces proud and sure. When the snow comes, everything goes. It's the worst winter any white man has ever seen in the Uplands. Some of the Iroquois head south.

"Neither heathen nor man can endure this," the Reverend Dunne says to Logan.

Logan's horses can't take the cold and there isn't anything to eat. There was hay in Champlain, but it was expensive and his horses hated it.

"Might be a good time to think about selling some of those noble equines to McGowan," the Reverend says.

"My ass," Logan says.

"Beg your assertion, sir?" the Reverend says.

"I'd rather sell my ass," Logan says.

There have always been Millers in Vermont. Logan's grandfather brought the first real horses over, huge chestnut colts, longhairs who looked wild-eyed and arrogant, promenading their massive penises on the mist-cooled Fort Dummer grass. The fillies came the next spring and the Millers owned every horse in the territory. The old man had bought them from a French-Spaniard named Teberre. Teberre liked the Iroquois' ascetic simplicity and their innate sense for the mercenary. They made him money that would have purchased the finest masonry in Avignon. In the end, though, they cut his hands and feet off, letting him sit on a pole—alive—for three days before the scalp was finally hammered off.

"McGowan's a decent man," the Reverend says. "His father was a Roundhead, bad-tempered—but still, for a Scot, he was decent."

Logan thinks of Lycidas, a pure black colt that in good times would've been worth the county and a bit more. "I love that fucking horse," he says to the Reverend Dunne.

The snow starts to get powderlike, *seeasueggu* the Algonquins who have been north, really north, call it. The cold is unbearable. The missionaries stop going into the Green Mountains to give the Indians communion.

Logan's best mare can no longer walk. He stays up with her for two nights, rubbing her legs and stomach. She staggers, does not eat, and is quiet. Her grandfather came from the stable of a Pahlavian prince. She knows how to die. She goes to sleep with regal stoicism. The other horses look at Logan.

"She was a queen," he tells them. He opens and drinks from the last bottle of scotch he has in the house and prepares a saddlebag, putting the bottle in. The ride to McGowan's is only an hour and a half, but the cold worries Logan. Near McGowan's place, Logan can see the gray-bearded Scotsman waving to him.

"You're a crazy man, to be out in this," McGowan says to Logan when Logan gets there. He still has a thick Scotch accent, and his eyes disappear when he smiles. The beard covers almost all of his face. "Let's put your horse inside, or we'll be eating him later," he says to Logan.

Inside, McGowan gives Logan a warm cup of apricot tea. "She makes that herself," he says, motioning to his woman. She is tall, her bosom full, and her skin more pink than is possible for any Scot to have. "She's from Scandinavia," he says. "Elizabeth," he says, and the woman curtsies quickly.

Logan takes her hand. "After the Queen Mother," he says.

"God, not that sot," the big Scotsman says. "After me mother," he says. "I hate the English. Inbreeders. Don't mean to offend," he says.

"I'm a Vermontan," Logan says.

"Good man, then, Logan," McGowan says. "No need to

talk to me wife, she doesn't speak a word of English. She's only been here a fortnight is all. I sent for her. I did a bit of the Jack Tar, you know."

Elizabeth smiles, offers Logan more to drink.

"I came to see if you're still interested in my horses," Logan says.

"Like a pup to an udder. You know well enough that I weep when I see those animals strutting by, their crowns on their hind legs," McGowan says.

"They're worth more than all the colonies put together," Logan says. He feels an unusual pulling in his chest. "I only want my six black colts, the six youngest fillies, and the horse I'm riding. That'll leave you fifty-eight, half of them colts. I averaged it out. I think twenty pounds a horse is a fair price."

"Have no doubt," McGowan says. "That's what I'll pay."

"No offer of your own?" Logan says.

"Fair is fair," McGowan says.

The two men drink.

"Me father was a whiskey maker," McGowan says.

"My own father was a minister," Logan says.

"I knew him. Sold me that white mare I had until two summers ago. Proper gentleman, never smiled," says McGowan.

"True. A man always about his horses," Logan says.

"No doubt," McGowan says. "What year were you born in?" he asks.

"Seventeen hundred," Logan says. "First of January."

"A new man for a new century," McGowan says. "Never thought of marrying?" he says.

"Never," Logan says.

"Women are good," McGowan says. "I like them quite a bit. I like the way they look when they are bathing."

"Only woman I've ever seen was an Indian one time, in the stream on my land," Logan says.

"Why, that can't be, Logan. Ye must have seen other women," McGowan says.

"Never have," Logan says.

"What'd she look like, then?"

"Dark. Large-breasted, strong," Logan says.

"You need to have a woman. Women are good," says McGowan.

"My mother died giving birth to me," Logan says.

"I feel for you, Logan, man." McGowan's face gets redder with every drink.

"I'll go and bring the first of those horses," Logan says. "I don't want to get caught in nightfall."

"I'll give you the money now," McGowan says.

"When the horses are all here," Logan says.

Before he saddles his horse, McGowan puts his arm on Logan's shoulder. "Logan, man, it's a hard thing, I know." He kisses Logan on the forehead.

"I'll be back," Logan says.

Logan's horses have never really known any other home. A few have been taken south, having been bought by Virginians. But Logan thinks Virginians stupid because, like their slaves, they slur their words. The horses are quiet while Logan ties them together.

Logan himself is unemotional. The liquor has worn off and he is cold. He looks at their teeth, rearranges their magnificent scrotal sacs, and squeezes the big muscular folds on their chests. He takes them across the snow toward McGowan's place. The whiskey has slowed him down and the hour is later than he thought it would be. He wonders about his grandfather, who he saw only at the end, when the man was dying, and about the old man's women—a wife and an Indian girl the old man had traded a terrifically wicked colt named Tybalt for.

At McGowan's place, Logan takes the horses in. He puts

blankets over all of them and lets them eat oats out of his hand. He knocks at the house and Elizabeth lets him in.

"Where's McGowan?" Logan says.

"You stay," Elizabeth says. "McGowan get horse *merde*," she says.

"Food," Logan says. "Horse *food.* There's the Queen's English, and there's McGowan's brigandry. Where is that Scotsman going to find hay and oats?" Logan says.

"Yes," Elizabeth says. "McGowan say you stay."

"It'll be dark soon," Logan says. "Let me take care of my horse and get my saddlebag."

Elizabeth makes some rolls and gets some apricot preserves. She is cooking something in a kettle over the fire. *"Kartoffel,"* she says. She gets some food for Logan. He is hungry and eats fast, drinking some whiskey from the bottle he left. After he eats, he sits by the fire. Elizabeth is sewing.

"When will McGowan be back?" Logan says.

"No," Elizabeth says.

Logan has no idea what the woman is talking about. He looks out the window. The cold seems to freeze the lights that come from town. Elizabeth comes to the window.

"Uhyre," she says.

In the dim light, Logan can see something moving in the snow. "Moose," he says to her.

Logan goes to the wall where McGowan has some muskets. He takes one and pours some powder into it. He loads it carefully. When he gets outside, the big bull moves away. It is dark and the animal is too far away for a clean shot, so Logan goes for a head shot. He misses. The bull slowly moves into the black.

Inside, Elizabeth is sewing again.

"No," Logan says to her. He sits on the floor and cleans out the Scotsman's gun. When he is finished, Elizabeth brings out some quilts and pillows for him.

"My father used to take me hunting when I was a child. This place was smaller then, not very many English," Logan says. "I used to imagine being alone out there all the time, just hunting and riding my horses."

"Yes," Elizabeth says. She kneels on the floor next to him. She kisses his hands. She stands and undoes her dress. In her underwear, she slowly unlaces her corset. She undoes her front. Her breasts are larger and whiter than the Indian woman's and she picks them up for him to see.

"I was the first person born in this century, in this county," Logan says.

Logan is up before the sun has completely risen. The snow is still bluish. The woman is still sleeping. Logan starts a fire and has a drink of whiskey with some rolls and preserves. Outside, the humidity has come back and the air has a sharp, loud sting to it. On his horse, Logan feels the first flakes of coming snow. His horse lets out a snort, and Logan pats his neck, calming him. The snow starts to come hard and fast. They go quietly for a while. Then the horse neighs loudly again, nostrils flared, its eyes red, like a man yelling, *"Come! Come, you motherfucker, come!"* **Q**

The Boys in the Highlands

I am on my knees and a man's hands are on my head.

"This," he says, referring to me and only me, "is your outside linebacker. He is your grace. Where he roams, he is a prince. He comes like God into a valley. This is the guy you want to bang your girl friends and mothers. He's Batman and Captain Marvel. He doesn't hand-hold cornerbacks, he transcends containment, his pain absolves, his shriek is refuge. Worship him and step to the mountain."

The man has tears in his eyes.

I am thirteen.

Some things that I have: a small apartment near the Surf Theatre, three thousand twelve records, Florida on my knees, an ass-breaking love of the Romantics, Helen.

The apartment has bay windows. The albums are stacked on their sides. I have the first one I ever bought, a collection of Christmas carols by the Berlin Girls' Choir on Deutsche Grammophon.

I had surgery on my knees my last year of ball. I was on Demerol and Michelob and I took my buck knife and carved along the scars—nothing too deep—cutting out the rest of Florida on both legs. The left one looks better.

Sometimes, I am a happy man.

I have this kid, he's in my English class. His name is Matt. He wants to write. After class, he comes to my office. You can see the Moraga hills out my window.

"I want something sweet, with a lot of carbonation, sugar, and caffeine pumping out of its ass, and I'll be happy," I say.

Matt looks at my wall. There's a picture of Unitas.

"He was great," he says.

"His testicles were diamond and his spit was nectar. Bring me something you've written by tomorrow," I say.

"Who do you like?" he asks.

"There are only Romantics," I say.

"Parts. I can give you my story in parts," he says.

"Fine," I say.

"Done," he says. "Hey, you want me to buy you a Coke or something?"

My mother always had to fight the weight. She always looked good, though, nice legs and everything.

I'm seventeen and during the off-season it comes for me, too. I take a piss and can't see my weiner.

I'm depressed.

I make a cheesecake.

My mom's living with this guy named Terrell. Terrell buys me a sleeping bag, a tent, backpack, fancy buck knife, boots.

"We'll hike and camp, it'll make you lean," Terrell says. Terrell is a high-school teacher, with a big, weird-sloping forehead. Terrell's wife comes over. She's not bad-looking, and she's not friendly.

We don't go camping.

I keep the knife and backpack, and sell everything else for thirty-six bucks.

Helen, wanting.

I run sprints—forties—on Saturday mornings. Helen watches me. I ran a four-five when I was with the Colts and had real legs. Death in a pair of cleats.

My legs get tight pretty quick, my ankles hurt, and I limp a little now. I put ice packs on my knees when I'm done. Helen rubs the cramps out of my quads and hams.

"Not so old," she says. She puts her head on my knee.

I was once a crashball man, who was a god, who'd been a kid, who begged the day to play ball like no one else.

I am now a stunt-bred zot-pastiche that'll do anything—
—anything—
—for this woman on my knees.

Coach Sanders used to block for Ernie Nevers. He's got this picture of the two of them standing together before the Notre Dame game when Nevers blasted the Four Horsemen. Coach Saunders has the biggest chest I've ever seen. There is strong, and there is strong.

"You're different now," he says, after moving me to linebacker. "You live outside of all of us. What you bless is refuge for your teammates."

Understand that I was once a free safety and that there is now—has always been—September grass too hot to sit on. I sit, exalted and a boy.

"You have to learn to wait. You watch, you wait, and then you explode and destroy," Coach Saunders says. He pats me on the head. "Go home now."

There is Una. There is her castle, her father, her suitor. Into their bliss comes a message from her former handmaiden, Shelley, now a captive awaiting death in the forest. An inexorable bond of loyalty bids Una leave and rescue her friend. The smitten Red-Crosse Knight, understanding the plight of honor, sends her off.

Una rides from the castle toward the forest, valley folding up behind her. Her white and rose-tinged breasts feel loved in her armor. She is erect and unblinking in her maiden-frenzy and determination. Her steed feels comforted in the milkiness of her hands. She is the grace of man.

At the forest's beginning, Una stands, hesitating.
She enters.

I was once a twin. My brother and me, identical and upside down, each one of us in our own little sacs. My brother stopped growing, then began to shrink. Sometimes one baby dominates in the fight for nutrition, and the weaker one doesn't make it.

I think about it: the two of us playing together, strongside and weakside, colossal warriors dispersing havoc and justice.

Things I'm scared of: forgetting that I've read Lermontov, some seventeen-year-old girl pouting and pointing tiny panties at me and asking, "Will you, will you?," AstroTurf, and my knees, God, *my knees.*

That's all.

The end of my senior year. I benchpress four-twenty-five. I'm juiced up—Deca going through me like blood—and the Colts are waiting. I have a buddy, Terry. He's an art major, spends his days taking down the women he paints and his nights taking down the women he can't paint. He's a little effeminate, worries a lot about his work, and calls me by my first name.

"Anthony," he howls.

He is in agony.

"I don't know what to tell you," I say. I give him a ride home. There are two girls sitting in front of his door.

He invites me in.

I thank him and say no.

My life into a backpack.

Terry comes to see me when I leave. He's in a car with a girl.

"Take care, buddy," he says. "Maybe Baltimore'll work out." He waves. "Art can never save you, you know," he says.

"It's hard to say," I say, and wave good-bye.

"Yes," I tell her, "Yes, I will," she looks at me, "Yes," I say, barely breathing, "Yes, I can, yes, I will."

Yes.

I hate my dreams.

It comes from the apartments across from me.
Bagpipes. Lost voices. A man and a woman.

On the first day of camp, the starting guard clips me.
He spits on me when I get up.

"You got a problem, rook?" he says.

Two plays later they run a sweep away from me. I'm two
hundred and twenty-three sublime pounds moving at full
speed. The guard turns and sees me just before I get there. He
gets this *look*—not really a look but more like a face movement—and it's the thing I play for, not to win, but for this.

I feel his collarbone go right away—but later, when they
tell me his shoulder's jelly, I'm a little surprised. I hear that
they waive him and he cries.

Backs see me and freeze. They hug the ball to their
bodies. I kick guys who cut me, punish guys who call me
names. Underneath piles, I ram fingers into eyes, necks,
groins. Where I go, pain looms. I hover, swift and angry. On
this fifty-by-one-hundred piece of earth, I cherish all things
given me.

I'm at two-fifty three weeks before camp. To cut
weight, I have toast, a raw egg, and orange juice for breakfast;
chicken vegetable soup and a beer for dinner. I pump in the
morning and run before I go to bed.

Byron used to balloon, getting miserable and stamping his
deformed and infected foot. He would starve himself, go into
seclusion, taking off to the Highlands or Aberdeen sometimes.
In Venice once, Teresa Guiccioli forbade the servants from
bringing him anything but biscuits and soda water.

Byron didn't scream. He sat half-dressed in a large chair

by the window, quiet and dark. It's no surprise that he lost his jest.

I call for a pizza, big and furious pieces of garlic on it.

Una, riding.

To her sides, the mystic verdant, unespied faeries in white linen, lost warriors. In the mythic black-soiled forest there is little trace of sun. It is a trippy place for a girl and her horse to be.

Her eyes see movement among the trees. Like the angel Gabriel putting up his wings for that last elusive roll for a seven, she darts toward it.

Shelley, tied to a horse. Her evil captor, Ido, lascivious and void of etiquette.

Una charging. Steel against steel. Ido using underhandedness. Una falling. Shelley riding away.

Walden is the dullest book I've ever read, and the pond is a dump. I hate Massachusetts, especially Boston. The way it looks, its smell, everything. The whole state gets on my last nut. We come into town to play in Foxboro.

I go to Cambridge to hear this lecture on Keats. The professor, a tall woman with black eyes named Dockmoor, isn't bad, but she spends too much time on Keats's lovers. Afterward, I take her to her apartment on Mr. Auburn.

I tell her that Massachusetts is a pit and to forget about Keats's women. She gets some imitation cognac and pours us glasses.

"What are you currently reading?" she says.

I tell her that I'm reading a book where this guy pours a glass of milk over his wife's hole and beats it into cream.

I tell her the title.

Helen and I are correcting papers on the couch when Matt comes over.

"Hey, I thought we could get toasted or something," he says. He has a pizza and a case of beer.

"Sure," I say.

I introduce him to Helen.

"Ain't she a babe?" I say.

"Ain't she a babe," Matt says.

"Rodriguez says you can really write," Helen says.

"Sentences," Matt says. "I can write some all right sentences."

"Rodriguez wants to save you," Helen says.

"People are into that," he says. "I just want to write a story, you know." He hands us beers. "Are you a Romantic too?" Matt says to Helen.

Rocklin, California. Forty-Niners' country. My knees are barely staying together. After the Colts cut me on Friday, I catch a flight out. I'm older than most of the linebackers in camp.

Some kid from Boise State looks at me like I'm a monument.

"Can I have your autograph?" he says. I give it to him. The other players make fun of him. At lunch they steal his dessert.

"You look like an old man," one of the coaches says to me.

It's a hundred and nine degrees. I feel my legs go. The desert is cruel. I am thirty years old.

There is the sound of only one bagpipe tonight.

We are cooking.

Somebody calls.

"My kid says you called him stupid," he says.

"Your kid is more than stupid," I say. "He's insipid." I smile at Helen. She holds up a skillet of mushrooms so I can see their sautéed glory.

"Look, you son of a bitch, I have a black belt," the guy says. "I'll kick your ass."

I turn away from Helen so she can't hear me. "I'm in the phone book," I say. "I don't have a black belt, but even at other people's games the rules are always my own, and when you get here, we'll play. Come."

The guy is quiet for a little bit. "I'll jack you up," he finally says, and hangs up.

"Smell," Helen says, holding out her mushrooms.

I smell.

"Yes," I say, "That's it."

I was once a god.

I know how to wait.

Helen is asleep. I grab a couple of rolls of quarters from my dresser. In the living room closet I find my old helmet. I take my sock off, unroll the quarters, and put them in the sock. I swing it over my head. I take my helmet and mace outside. I sit on the porch steps.

When I played with the Colts, I used to sit in the bleachers at Vet Memorial after the game. I could see the houses across from the stadium, people wrapped in blankets, sipping beer and sitting in lawn chairs. There was always this sense of in-completeness—no matter how good I was. I've always wanted completion.

Something.

Anything.

I swing the sock.

Strapped to a table, the naked Una, awaiting death.

Unreal beauty, soft V of hair coming from between her legs. There's a terror that brings the sheer deafening sound of injustice with it. It is the nefarious and very im-polite Ido.

Like the sound of steel wire cutting through a lover's last discordant sigh, there is Shelley, her penis-shaped sword held high over her head. She runs to Una's side, hair and breasts fly in synchronized free verse, her dong-saber whirrs.

Ido is astonished, but his never-hesitant cutlass is at his side.

There are thrusts and swipes. There is blood. Shelley falls to her knees, but with one final graceful and prodigious blow she removes Ido's head.

It is messy. It is sad.

Life ebbing from Ido.

Shelley throws her sword to Una, who cuts herself free.

Una runs to Shelley, our sabreur, and holds her.

Una lifts her breast and gives Shelley a final succor.

Shelley, dying; Una, weeping.

This is how it will be: I will be standing by the curb outside, in front of the school building, waiting for somebody, Helen maybe. This car will go by, and Matt'll be in the passenger side. There'll be a girl in the back and her arms will be around Matt's shoulders.

"Hey, Mr. R.," they'll say.

Matt will hold his hand out.

I'll shake it.

Other cars will go by and all those things I have always been willing to wait for will come, all rolled up into one. **Q**

Out the Window

There's a cowboy on the corner of Columbus with a sewing machine. I watch him from my window up on the second floor, past my Christmas tree and lights. The parakeets are out, sitting on a towel. The sewing machine looks to me weird out in the street where people pass by carrying normal things, like salad containers and ironing boards. I can't take the suspense, and lock up, and go downstairs in my red scarf and coat, to check this guy out. We end up taking a cab to the Dunkin' Donuts at Penn Station and I'm choosing from a tray of lemon custard, and some mother with purse and dirty hands screams: "Muffin! Give me a muffin!" I get my donut, napkin, and wax bag, and thank the cowboy. Nothing nicer than a new donut, and that first bite.

He asks me to take a walk down Seventh with him, and I think sure, why not? So we walk, and I eat. He carries the sewing machine, and I hear his spurs are scraping the sidewalk like.

We take a turn, pass some places, come to a flower shop and stairs next to it, and we climb up into a building that stinks. Down a hall to the side is a door. Cowboy unlocks it and when the door opens, first thing I smell is soup.

Cowboy takes off the cowboy hat and he puts on a cap with a name written on it. He puts the machine down on a table and calls for Lily.

"Lily! Lily! Lily!" he's calling out, and finally this woman comes out of what's probably the bedroom.

"Found a machine," Cowboy says to her.

I don't like soup, never did, but I mostly eat the crackers they give me from tiny crushed packets.

"Looks good," Lily says.

"I guess I can fix it," Cowboy says.

"You can fix anything," Lily says. "You got the touch."

"Guess so," Cowboy says.

Cowboy's got on the late news, all worried, chin in his hands. Lily's sewing. I'm thinking, here I am at a door waiting to say good-bye to people.

"Good-bye," I say.

Cowboy looks tired and sad.

Then he tells me something I later tell my parakeets while I'm looking back out the window.

"You know what is the worst thing that can happen to you in your life?" Cowboy says to me.

"Nothing," Cowboy answers, and closes the door. **Q**

Wall, Plinth, Merlon, Talus, Donjon Tower

The silence awakens him. Nearly an hour after winter sunrise the seacoast is still dark, shadowed by mountains to the east. Yet in this hour, and only in winter, the stones of the ruined fortress begin to give off a white glow. The tower, the sandstone walls crumbling like a stairway into the sea, shimmer with a light that can be seen for miles against the black of the mountain shadow. Native fishermen call the place Bah'm Adeem, Old Thumb, and mark their positions by the glow of its stones.

Except for the regular break of the surf, it is quiet in this hour after first light. The dogs have stopped their racket, the crying gulls are far out to sea. This silence wakes him every morning. In his years at the prison camp of Bah'm Adeem he has become used to noise. All day there is the noise of men working, the convicts with shovels, the Frenchmen shouting out numbers to be written down, and, far off, fishermen chanting as they pull in their nets. At night it is dogs mostly, the yapping and snarling of village strays. Too, a roomful of sleeping men is never quiet. So in this hour when the dogs are away—gone God knows where—and the men hush to just the taking in and letting out of breath, Alexio Jowah sits straight up on his pallet. This morning his chest is tight with impatience. But like the gleam of the stones, the silence will not last. When the first rays of true sunlight break over the mountain, the muezzin of Harsoun will begin it all again with the call to prayer. The stricture in Alexio's chest will loosen against the urgings of his dreams, and his mother's voice will subside, be lost once more in the noise of people working, the noise of dogs—come back from God knows where—barking again.

Now he hears the distant voices of the fishermen in their

boats. They throw out nets and pull them in, chanting as they pull "El-ee-sah! El-ee-sah!" He recalls Le Conseiller d'Affaires Archaiques asking two older convicts, once fishermen, if they knew what the word meant. They said that they did not, only that it brings fish. Their fathers and grandfathers who taught them the workings of nets and boats taught them also to chant. So Le Conseiller told the men, and the other convicts who stopped digging to listen, about how Elissa was the name of the queen who worshipped the little clay Fat Woman found three years ago at Bah'm Adeem. It was in the trench by the north wall. Alexio remembered the Frenchmen on their hands and knees, digging her out with their fingernails. She stood on a small stair, hands to her breasts, giving milk to the little mud men below her.

"So you see," Le Conseiller told them, "how everything we find here concerns your people."

Although Le Conseiller spoke Arabic with the accent and in the dialect of the Egyptians, the convicts could make him out. They pretended interest and called him *baak,* your honor. Listening is easier than digging.

But when Le Conseiller was gone, the two convicts laughed. Alexio Jowah knew why. He had heard fishermen talking before, and the concern of their people was not the Fat Woman. *Il kabl ma b'himna,* they say here, and not just here but in every place that people speak Arabic: The past does not concern us. And the future? *Min Allah,* from God.

Alexio gets up from his pallet and goes to the open doorway. He waits there until the guard at the landward gate notices him and nods. The guard watches him go in the dim light from the shelterhouse to the privy holes. Only when Alexio is ready, trousers down and squatting, will the guard turn away. Alexio hurries. When he is finished, he signals with a cough. The guard turns back. Alexio waves his arm toward the sea bank. They have an understanding. If he rises early enough, Alexio is permitted to sit a while gazing at the sea, pressing with his hand against his chest, free for those few minutes before the muezzin calls out to Allah and everyone gets up. The guard nods again, watching Alexio step by step until he sits down facing the white sea. Far off, the fishing boats are passing slowly into a mist. The men are crying out to Elissa the way their fathers taught them to do.

The sea has turned a light gray now, and mist hides the fishing boats completely. The glow of the stones vanishes with the coming of daylight. The glow fades to the flat simple colors of sandstone and of limestone.

". . . Here, *beneath* means *before*," Le Conseiller would explain whenever a new gang of convicts arrived. A hole somewhere (but where he doesn't say) and sweet water.

"Here," Le Conseiller would tell the newcomers, "beneath the sandstone and limestone, there is basalt. Beneath the basalt, and so before the basalt, we found marble debris; and below that, red granite. Beneath it all, before it all, there is mud-and-straw baked hard. And, somewhere, the hole.

"The hole was first.

"All around there was desert, but here was sweet water and the sea, and here too were trees, growing wild like a gift from the Fat Woman they worshipped—olive, pomegranate, fig, cedar, date palm. As in other places, at Ras Melaikhee and Juffaid, the hole was dug first. It was shelter, a place to cook or make sacrifice. Then mud was mixed with straw and the tents were struck forever."

"And the hole?" Alexio had asked the first time he heard all this.

"Gone. And long before this was built."

"Gone how, *baak?*"

"Crushed under the weight of stone on stone. Or filled in on purpose to make room for other things. Red granite, marble, basalt—all are foundation for what stands now, the sandstone and limestone work of Crusaders.

"But the hole, *ya baak?*"

"Gone, Jowah. Caved in or filled in on purpose."

And now the sun, sudden, as after the passing of a large cloud. It turns the sea from gray to deep blue. You can watch it happen. Below, near the tumbled stones of the west wall, the light strikes something that Alexio did not notice there yesterday. He shifts a little to see. Between two stones a dog lies dead, paws up and stiff. It is miserable-looking, skinny, its fur in thick, mangled clumps. There are patches of gray skin on the hindquarters. Its tail, like the tail of a rat, has no fur at all. Alexio turns away and spits for luck, but his mind remarks the picture. What legs spread to bear that? And those legs, wherever they are now, they do not remember it. The papa that spread them does not care, does not even know. You could stick his nose in that fur and he would wonder What trick now? Roll over? Play dead? This is my meal maybe? When dogs say good-bye to their pups, it is good-bye forever.

The muezzin at Harsoun calls long and wailing. It is Friday. Alexio will ask more about the tower. Last Friday he got Le Conseiller to promise to show him the inside of the tower, where no convict has ever been permitted to work. All week Alexio has fought impatience with a hand against his chest.

The morning noise is beginning. Alexio can hear the shouts of the guards rousing the convicts in the shelterhouse. He gets up and walks quickly back down the rise. He does not want to cause trouble for the landward guard. The full disk of the sun is now over the mountain. Alexio squints into it as he walks to where the convicts are lining up for soap and shaving. Five razors are counted, passed out with bowls of water, then passed on to the next five convicts and then on to the next until shaving is over and the razors are counted again. The line is long and slow. It is hard to keep clean here. Alexio has had the lice two or three times each year he has been at Bah'm Adeem.

Even the guards get it. Bookra never minded the lice. He said once that the sheikh of his tribe cultivated lice in the hair of his head as a sign of wisdom.

The line shuffles. Talking is not permitted until after breakfast. Alexio waits only for the soap and water to wash. When his turn comes, he refuses the razor. He has not shaved for months so that when the time is upon him he will be ready.

Because after all the thinking, the key was at last given to him in that first vivid dream of Mama. He dreamed she was sitting in the front room of the apartment above Papa's store on Monroe Street. It was Mama as she used to look long ago before the betrayals, eyes bright with laughter before Papa ran off to go back to the old country, before her brother, her own blood, sealed Alexio in this place and abandoned him here to dream of that laughing face. Cards were laid out on the table for *baserah*: the Old Man, the Lady, and the Lad who trumps them both. Picking up the Lady, Mama said in her loud voice, louder in the dream, "If you are a plumber, My Eyes, look for the hole." She pointed to the window, but instead of Monroe Street, there was the sea pouring in. Alexio awoke startled in that white, silent hour just after the sun has risen. That was more than a year ago. Since then there have been many dreams—and Mama is in all of them, but none has been as clear, as strong, as that one. It was a true-dream. How else would Mama know about the hole? And besides, Alexio is afraid of the sea. Alone on the boat trip back across the Atlantic he was sick the whole time. Yet if the guards were to read his mind, were to take away the soap and basin, were to chain him, throw him into the sea chained, it would be better than this. For even so Alexio Jowah would make his way to Beirut, would climb the Lebanon to Ras il Missihiyeh, would go all the way to his uncle's house, would find his father and uncle then, and avenge the honor of his mother.

Chained and drowned and a ghost, Alexio Jowah would still get to them.

. . .

Inside, more than a dozen men lay snoring and moaning on wooden pallets. Someone in the back could not stop coughing. Alexio groped in the half-darkness to an empty pallet. The wood of the pallet was filthy. The whole place stank. It smelled like garlic and urine.

But he could not sleep. His mind was too busy for that. He listened past the snoring to the sounds outside, the guards calling to one another and, farther away, the dogs.

Then, close to his pallet, Alexio heard someone breathing deeply, but not like in sleep. There was a rustling sound of movement. He looked, but in the darkness he could make out only a shadow that seemed to be moving closer. He pretended he was asleep.

"Bookra," a voice said in Arabic. "Tomorrow."

Alexio kept his eyes shut, his breathing deep and steady.

"Stop pretending," the voice whispered next to his ear. "Don't you know what they're going to do to us tomorrow?" The accent was not Lebanese. Sudani maybe, or Philistini. Alexio squinted a look at him. The face was black, and not from the light. A gold square dangled from the man's neck, a Koran the Moslems wear the way Christians wear crosses.

"Tomorrow?" Alexio's voice was small next to the black man's, even in whisper. Alexio thought of his father—a sudden, crazy thought—who was always black bending over Alexio's bed at night.

"Tomorrow they will hang us," the black man said.

"But not me." Alexio's voice was shaking. The black man talked like someone who knew. He put his hand on Alexio's arm, and suddenly Alexio trusted no one but him.

"You, too, *ya musq'een*," the black man said. "Every one of us." Then the black man made a noise, abrupt and deep, like the bark of a big dog. This started Alexio crying.

"Oh, please, Jesus," Alexio said in English.

And while he was crying, the black man struck Alexio on the head with a piece of board and quickly yanked off his shoes.

Alexio did not know why the black man had hit him. It was not a hard blow. He did not faint from it. "Dear Jesus Christ." Alexio did not care about the shoes. If the black man wants to hang tomorrow with American shoes on his feet, so what? Because Alexio now saw his own death as something that would truly, truly happen. "Oh, oh, oh, oh." He used to look at his hands when he was little. He used to look at them and say, "Dead, dead." He used to look at his face in Mama's mirror and say "Dead, dead, dead, dead." Until the idea sank in. Nothing else would matter after he did that. Nothing.

He could barely see the black man at the foot of his own pallet now, struggling to put on the shoes.

"They didn't hang you yet," Alexio said to show he was not afraid.

"*Bookra*," the black man said.

That was the black man's name in the shed. The men in the shed called him that because it was what the black man always said: Tomorrow they will shoot us. Tomorrow they will hang us.

"I don't care," Alexio said in English.

"Tomorrow," the black man was saying, "eat only *laban*, the sour yoghurt. At both meals put a pinch of this in the *laban*." He showed Alexio a spoonful of white powder wrapped in paper. "It will heal you," and the black man made a sign with his hand to mean very fast, the hand opened, then snapped closed to a fist. Like catching flies.

"What is it?"

The powder had no smell. Poison, Alexio thought. So they can be rid of me. No, not of me. They don't know me. But rid of my stink, yes. Rid of the noises I make in the night, yes.

"Poison?" Alexio asked.

"No," the black man said. "But if you want poison, I can get that, too. This is opium. Fast," and he made the gesture again, like catching flies.

"Why? You don't know me."

"Is your name really Jowah?" The black man seemed to be holding back a laugh as he said the name.

"Yes."

"Then, say I know him. Say he is a friend of mine."

"Who?"

"Jowah." This time Bookra laughed out loud.

"Ulyas Jowah, my father?"

"No. This one would be much older."

"A relative of mine?"

"Aren't all Jowahs related?"

"My father says so."

"Well, then." Bookra crawled back to his own pallet and bunched himself in the blanket.

"Bookra?" Alexio leaned forward to see the black man. "Is it evening?"

"It is morning."

"Are you a Sudani?"

Bookra did not move beneath the blanket. When he spoke there was a smile in his voice, a kind of amusement. "Yes. Say I am a Sudani."

"You're not a Sudani? A Berber, then?"

"Say I am a Berber."

When the truck from Beirut first arrived at Bah'm Adeem, each new convict was stripped naked, searched, and sent to the bathing stalls for delousing. Afterward, the chief officer of the guards spoke to them about fair treatment, hard work, and the penalty for escape attempts. Le Conseiller gave his speech about something being here to start with, about how *beneath* means *before,* and they were put to work digging a trench along the foundations of the citadel's north wall.

The winter rain made it slow work, but the Frenchmen made it even slower. They had the convicts going through every handful of mud and clay to be sure that no piece of pottery, no fragment of bronze would be lost. Above ground and below, the French overlooked nothing, measuring this stone or that wall, measuring the pillars, the shadows of the pillars at sunrise and sunset. They weighed pebbles and marked them with white numbers, burned them with acid. They stared through magnifiers at scratches in the rock. The convicts struck sandstone after a month's digging. Between the French and the winter rain, it took three months more to reach the black bitumen four feet below.

Alexio worked hard and did not complain. Now, Alexio thought, it was best to make no trouble of any kind; to work hard and show them that he was no criminal.

In work, all the convicts were alike, but in free time there had formed small, clearly designated circles, and these circles had their leaders. It was nothing set down; it happened. The shore Christians, mostly Melkites and Greek Orthodox, kept to themselves and did not mix with the Maronite Christians from the mountains. Shi'ia Moslems had their own faction, as did the Sunni and the Druze. There was even a separate circle made up of outsiders, who had no other bond except that they were outsiders.

Bookra did not go into any circle. And not because he was black, Alexio noted. The outsiders had blacks, and so did the Sunni, but Bookra did not go to either of them. No, it was because he had a way of saying crazy things to anyone who was standing within earshot, things that would stop people and make them stare at him. Once, during the noon meal, a group was talking about executions. Bookra came and sat nearby; he was not being spoken to, unnoticed, actually, except for Alexio, who had looked his way a moment. Yet Bookra interrupted what they were saying. He said, "Talk of executions always reminds me of the Bazaar Khan al Khalileh in Cairo where I saw them making crosses for sale to the Christians. One man had wooden crosses laid out on a workbench. The basket next to him was full of little gold-painted Christs with their arms out like this."

Bookra held his arms out and paused. The others said nothing. Some continued to eat, ignoring him on purpose.

"Fast, like a machine," Bookra said, "this man would fish a Christ from the basket, spit a tack into his hand, take his hammer, and nail the Christ to the cross—one hand, the other hand, feet—just like that."

One man said "the Yazid," and made the palm-up sign against the evil eye.

Then Alexio stood with the others and began to walk away. Bookra followed him, saying, "Wasn't that funny, *ya ibni*? Think about it! It's funny if you think about it."

Ibni?

My son?

Alexio hurried his step so the others would not think Bookra meant him when he said *ibni*.

In the day Bookra worked next to Alexio. At meals he sat near the Maronite group, breaking into what they were talking about with a loud laugh or another crazy story. In the evenings before sleep, Bookra sat listening while Alexio told him of Mama, of how his family first went to America, of the years on Monroe Street, about Toledo and how he, Alexio Jowah, had become a plumber there.

Bookra listened in silence mostly, twisting the iron bracelet around and around with his fingers, or looking out the open door of the shelterhouse.

By day the rock turned soft—breccia, Le Conseiller called it—crumbling against the shovel and, deeper, against the weight of a man's hand. With the heat of summer, Le Conseiller and two government assistants remained to direct the digging. Again, hard labor turned into the drudgery of sifting each handful of the gritty rock lest something be overlooked.

By autumn, the rains slowed things even more. A bellows pump was set up to drain the ditch, but the canvas hose took in mud with the water. At the end of each day the length of it had to be cleared, and each day there was more rain. And the mud too had to be pressed and sifted through wire screening.

All winter the convicts were black to their necks. The rain chilled them to the bone and one day there was even snow. Alexio remembered how his father used to hate the winters in Toledo, how he never got used to the snow. In the middle of January Alexio's father would come in from shoveling the alley behind the store so deliveries could be made. The man would stamp the snow from his shoes in the back room. It would be dark outside, though only suppertime. Upstairs, Mama would have the food waiting—rolled grape leaves or lamb ground in cracked wheat or lemony chicken stuffed with pine nuts, and the man would eat while Mama and Alexio would kneel in front of him and pull the wet shoes from his feet.

By spring they had passed the bituminous layer and found slabs of red granite. Most probably a floor, Le Conseiller told them. Maybe even the work of Thutmose himself when he had brought his armies here.

"So permanent a floor," Le Conseiller said as he knelt to touch it, "so polished once. It was floated down the Nile, cut and finished and loaded again for transport to this place. At Baalbek, pillars the size of tall trees were dragged across two mountain ranges, the Lebanon and the Antilebanon."

The convicts at his back listened the way children listen to their father when he is talking business. One of them made jokes with his eyes and got the others to snorting and biting the backs of their hands.

"Here, *beneath* means *before*," Le Conseiller would explain whenever a new gang of convicts arrived. Alexio had heard it all many times already. He had been assigned to special duties because of his good memory and the way he had of doing practical things carefully and according to directions, his willingness to cooperate and learn. Le Conseiller depended on him to keep close to new men and to watch over their work. So Alexio had heard it often, *beneath, before.*

"Beneath means before. Something here to start with, something to build on when the others came. A hole somewhere and sweet water. Here, beneath the sandstone and limestone, there is basalt. Three years ago we struck basalt in the trench by the north wall. Beneath the basalt, and so before the basalt, we found marble debris; and below that, red granite. Beneath it all, before it all, there is mud-and-straw baked hard. The mud-and-straw was first. (Now he will tap his cane once, maybe two times against a stone.) All around there was desert, but here was sweet water and the sea, and here too were trees, growing wild like a gift from the Fat Woman they worshipped—olive, pomegranate, fig, cedar, date palm. (And sometimes he will say peach, apricot, lemon, banana.) As in other places, at Ras Melaikhee and Juffaid, the hole was dug first. It was shelter, a place to cook or make sacrifice. Then mud was mixed with straw and the tents were struck forever. They built houses, a fort, surely a temple. She too took form from this mud. (He will say her names—Astarte, Tanit, Il Im, Elissatha.) In time the hole was abandoned or used for storage. The others, when they came, may even have opened it to the sea for a sewer. (But where, *baak*?) After them, still others came, taking what they found and making something else of it, making another temple probably, and then a fortress; certainly it was once a granary, a stable once, then again a fortress and again a fortress and, because of the Mediterranean on three sides, *again* a fortress. Red granite, marble, basalt—all are foundation for what stands now, the sandstone and limestone work of Crusaders. And because laid so long ago, it is a deep foundation, bearing well through earthquakes and wars the weight of wall, plinth, merlon, talus, and donjon tower. Then the last source of sweet water dried up, and men could no longer live here. The citadel of Bah'm Adeem was last used as a garage for the armored vehicles of a Turkish garrison from Harsoun."

"And the hole?" Alexio asked every time he heard this.

"Gone. Long before this was built."

"Gone how, *baak*?"

"Crushed under the weight of stone on stone. Or filled in on purpose to make room for other things."

Even at the first Alexio could see that. The stones along the seaward wall were not put together the same. Below, even the stone itself is different, black quarry-rock where you scraped away the moss. You did not need a magnifying glass or acid or little silver weights to know that others came and took and built, and that still others followed. Le Conseiller was a smart man, but he was no plumber. The people who built and tore down and built, they were plumbers. And plumbers do not fill a hole they can use. They are respectful of it, they watch that weight does not crush. In Toledo they even added segments to old holes. When the plumbers found sewer walls still shored up with wood, the plumbers did not fill the hole because it was rotten—they tore out the wood and put in brick. Alexio had helped them do it. And when they started using tile, he helped with that, too.

The convicts eventually left the trench to begin digging at the foundations of the citadel's south wall. Alexio worked, thinking only of what was before him—the shovel, the dirt.

The noise roused the camp and started the dogs howling. Afterward, the whole business had to be written down from beginning to end. The chief officer of the guards said that procedures demanded a written report, and also that the report be read aloud. At dawn muster, the Arab sergeant read it as if it were a list of the day's chores:

"An hour before daylight, the convict al Dahab (*so that was Bookra's name*) slipped past the stations of both guards at the landward gate. After which, he was able to crawl undetected to the east corner of the wire-line. There, he cut a hole in the wire. While attempting to crawl through the hole, he was discovered by a third guard. When the prisoner gave no response to the guard's challenge, indeed continuing to struggle through the hole in the wire, he was shot at and struck twice. He died soon after."

Bookra's corpse had been left where it was, half in and half out of the hole in the wire, so everyone at muster could see it. After dismissal, four convicts were told to take it to a shed.

That night Alexio lay back on his pallet like a sick man. When he awoke, it amazed him that he could have slept, amazed him more that he was hungry when he awoke. During the day his mind concentrated on other things: this shovel, this meal, this man's face. At night it was Mama and Bookra again; again it was all a jail, and there was only one way out. Again, his strength was gone, and he lay back to sleep. But the sea began to make its noise, and Alexio awoke startled in that white, silent hour of dawn at Bah'm Adeem.

Alexio catches sight of the white suit near the landward wall. Le Conseiller is on his knees, looking at something. More beneath and before. More someone built on what someone else left behind. Anybody who eats chick-peas in the morning and farts in the afternoon knows that much. For more than a year Alexio had pretended ignorance so that he would hear it all.

"The walls are European," Le Conseiller would only say. "The tower, the lower part at least, is Arab. The foundations are Byzantine."

"And the hole, *ya baak*?"

"Gone, Alexio. Caved in or filled in on purpose."

"*Ya baak!*"

Le Conseiller does not look up.

"*Ya baak!*" Alexio looks down and prepares his face for the show of wonder.

"Yes, Jowah?" Le Conseiller says it like a teacher.

"Today is Friday, *baak.*"

Le Conseiller raises his eyebrows to show that he does not understand.

"Today the tower."

"Did we say today, Lexi?"

Alexio waits before speaking, counts a slow four to himself. "But if you are very busy—"

"Come with me," Le Conseiller says.

He begins to open the gate himself, and a guard rushes to help him.

"Tell me," Le Conseiller says, stopping a few yards from the tower's thick base, "who built this wall?"

"The French, *baak*. The Crusader soldiers."

"Yes, Lexi." Le Conseiller touches the wall. "Do you know when?"

Alexio shrugs his shoulders. "Long ago."

"How long? Before you were born? Before your father?"

Alexio shrugs again, longer this time, a slow count of three.

"Lexi," Le Conseiller smiles, one eye half squinted, "this was built more than seven hundred years before your father was born."

"No!"

"Most truly taught. It was under Geoffrey de Giles that the Franks built this wall and added the tower's top two stories." Le Conseiller taps the wall lightly with the tip of his stick. "But look carefully at these stones."

"White stone." Alexio shifts to one foot.

"Smooth stone, Lexi." Le Conseiller swings the stick down to knee level. "And here?"

"The stones are pointed." A donkey could tell so much. But to stop the show of wonder would be to stop everything.

"The points give the wall strength against battering. These stones were here before Sir Geoffrey. And below us, to the waterline and deeper, is basalt set in thick mortar. You see, Lexi, before the Franks there were the desert Arabs."

"*Lah*!"

"Most truly taught."

"Ya salaam."

"Look now at the mortar. Look closely," Le Conseiller says.

Alexio kneels down. Le Conseiller stoops next to him and scrapes his thumbnail along the line of mortar. He opens his palm to show the white chips.

"Seashell?"

"No, Lexi, pieces of marble."

"La-ah!" To stretch it out, to pause in the middle before going on, is to let all the wonder of the word come out.

"Most truly taught. We know from this that Romans were here before the Moslems. We have found the source of the marble where the convicts are digging now. It was a temple—at least some of us think so—to Magna Mater, the Great Mother."

Alexio cocks his head the way he has seen dogs do.

"The statue, Lexi."

"The Fat Woman?"

"The same. She was for a long time popular among the eastern legions. But the statue is older than they. Even before the Romans, there were others. And always there was something to start with, something to build on when the others came."

"Sweet water?"

"Most truly taught, Lexi."

Alexio looks down a moment. This is like talking to a little boy, the old man calling him Lexi.

"And a hole to start with, *baak*?"

"Yes. At Ras Melaikhee and at Juffaid—"

The sea wind has shifted and flies are coming in with the first of the day's heat. Alexio crouches at the wall, swatting at the flies as he listens, pretending wonder even at things he already knows—*lah,* and *ya salaam*—while Le Conseiller takes things back to the beginning, to when those first ones came from the deserts of the south.

"And then the others started coming, Ezekiel's foreigners.

More and more came—Bedouin, Hyksos, Amorite, Hittite, Egyptian, Assyrian, Hebrew, Babylonian, Mesopotamian, Persian, Ethiopian, Greek, Indian, Turk, Macedonian, Italian, Byzantine, Mongol, Mameluke, Russian, German, Englishman, Spaniard, Swede, Hungarian, Frenchman. . . ."

"Tell me, *baak*, here they fought, ate, slept, drew water, but where did they shit? Over the walls?"

"Of course not, Lexi," Le Conseiller says. "To do so would be to invite pestilence. No, Lexi, they had latrines."

"Show me," Alexio Jowah says.

The food line is shuffling slowly toward the garlic smell of the kitchens. Alexio does not enter the line. To eat now would be the worst mistake, his death for certain. Instead, he returns to the tower and sits down alone in its shadow to rest himself and wait.

A village stray comes near. Its tail is stubbed, probably bitten off when it was a pup. "Papa!" Alexio calls to it. "You, Papa!" But the dog does not come closer.

"Uncle, then?" Alexio calls.

He throws a stone for the dog's face. The dog bolts a short distance and then turns, fur up, staring at Alexio in nervous readiness. Alexio picks up another stone. The dog does not run away. Instead, it snarls, crouches as if to leap at him. Alexio lowers his hand and drops the stone.

It could be death.

In the light of the torch he looks down at his hands.

Dead, dead, he thinks to ready himself, dead, dead, dead.

He strikes once with the spade, and water bursts out, gushes into his face. He strikes again. Water fills the space around him. He can feel its force begin to push him back. The torch is gone, swept somewhere behind him. He lets it go and works frantically in the darkness. Trapped water or the sea, there is no way to tell. It is hard to thrust the spade through the water. There is no room. He digs his knees and elbows into the muck, but still he is slipping. Only from the wrists and forearms, he thinks, and he strikes again, forearms and wrists into the thrust. The spade glances aside. Rock? He takes air and dives, claws downward with his fingers into the whipping dark green light—this is not trapped water! This is the hole somewhere, opened to the sea for a sewer.

His hands grasp not rock but a grid of iron spikes.

And the spikes flake against his touch.

He pushes.

The center gives like a rotted window screen. Again he takes air, dives, and begins to squeeze himself through, holding the air in his cheeks and stomach.

Finding its level, the water slows to the strong push and suck of the surf's tow, and the suction shoots him out like a stone.

The current pushes back against him.

All motion stops.

He hangs in the green quiet.

I am dying, he thinks, it is like this.

He screams—"Mama!"

Bubbles explode from his mouth, and he hurls to the surface, to air. Never mind what hurts, his stomach, his chest and sides from the iron spikes. He has come through the hole with his life, and they will never forget him, Alexio Jowah, who dug through the shit of all of them—Phoenician, Egyptian, Crusader, and Turk. **Q**

In the Wash

"Oh, stop it now—just stop it!" the mother said.

"Please, please, just let me stay here and watch," the little girl said.

"Shame on you!" the mother said.

"Oh, please, please, it's too scary out there," the little girl said. The little girl was looking at the wringer-washer letting loose from its bottom a stream of dirty water that looked to her like a stream of siss, as if the wringer-washer were making a siss that her mother was broom-sweeping into the drain in the middle of the basement.

"Do you want me to spank you?" her mother said. "Because if you don't scoot now, I will!" the mother said, taking the little girl by the hand to the door that led out to the garage and then leaving her there.

"Go! Go on!" the mother said.

So the little girl made her way over the slippery black splashes on the floor of the garage and out into the yellowy morning, cutting across the driveway and stepping up through the spiky rock garden to the grassy part of the backyard, where she saw the sheets hanging up like the white walls of something, the little girl thought, of something—anything—safe that she could be inside of. And this is what she did, got herself inside of them, stepping between the hanging sheets, and feeling the sun pat her on the top of her head as if approving of her cleverness.

Oh, it was a wonderful thing being safe inside the sheets and smelling the smells they had!—the wet and soapy smell mixing with the hot sun smell. So she lay down on the ground, feeling the grass fingering her back through her shirt, and squinted up at the sun shimmers glistening on the sheets and caught sight of the clothespins standing guard over the sheets and over the rest of the wash and probably, like little soldiers, even over the whole backyard.

It was then that the little girl understood there was nothing out in the yard that could scare her so long as she kept herself inside of the sheets, nothing that could probably even find her here—not even the things that lived under the sandbox or over in the forsythia bushes next to the fence or over there in the trees where the roots came crawling at you like nightmares on the ground.

Oh, it was glorious, being so safe!

How lucky she was to be hidden in the wash!

The little girl got to her feet and began prancing and strutting up and down the grassy rows between the sheets. She pumped her arms. She stuck her elbows out. She marched up and down, so wonderfully in charge of where she was!

But then something hideous happened!

It was an outrage, the sudden insult to her flesh!

For a small wind had made the sheets shake themselves as if they had got angry with her—and then, before the little girl could get away, get her arm back down to her side where it would be safe, a rush of wet linen flapped out at her and licked at her elbow.

Oh, it was horrible, horrible, horrible!

It felt to the little girl more horrible than anything she could ever have imagined, the thing probably trying to slither up to her neck to get up at her face and to stick its fingers in her nose and suffocate her to death.

She knew it was going to happen!

She just knew it!

So she started to go faster, to get away, but she felt the sheets watching for her, getting ready to close in on her for good, their filthy wet breath screwing into the naked place at the back of her neck.

Now she ran!

She could not stand it anymore—she had to, she just had to—so she just ran!

In the kitchen, she saw that there was no one there who could help her, so she kept on running, keeping her eyes fastened on the speckled linoleum, glimpsing up at the stove and at the refrigerator just to make sure they were not coming after her. But neither of them was moving to come after her themselves—they only just stood there, shouting, "Get her! Get her!"

When she got to the open door of the basement, she looked down at the down-spilling stairs and at the dark place under the banister and at the terrible dark spaces you could see between each of the steps.

The basement!

Oh, God, the basement!

But then she heard the things in the kitchen getting ready to come after her, a kind of ghostly laundry thing that was right there behind her back, and it was whispering, "Push her, give her a push!"

She fell.

She stumbled forward and fell, clattering down the steps until she had caught hold of something—the banister!—and hung there, helpless for an instant, screaming.

She screamed, "Mother, Mother, help, help!"

And her feet slipped off the stairs and now she was really dangling there, the black spaces behind the steps breathing on her legs with their disgusting cold breath.

"Mother!" the little girl screamed.

The oil burner!

She could see the oil burner standing down there in the hazy dark. It was like a sleeping thing, with pipes that stuck out from it and that snaked everywhere across the ceiling and the floor. But just beyond the oil burner she could see a yellow light coming from the laundry room.

Oh, God, her mother was in there!

Oh, Mother, Mother, she wanted to call out again, but the little girl suddenly realized that if she did call out again, she might wake up the oil burner. Yes, yes, of course—it would be crazy to risk arousing the oil burner. But how, on the other hand, could she stay where she was?

It was impossible!

Her hands hurt so, and the pits deep in the crooks of her arms hurt so—and just behind her, she was sure of it now, she could hear the flapping of the hideous ghostly wash. Yes, yes, it was getting closer. The sheets! Oh, God! She let go of the banister and dropped down to the floor of the basement, and scrambled away like a crab, crawling like an animal now, going on her hands and knees to the light. "Mama!" the little girl shrieked when she saw her mother. Clambering around the ugly drain in the middle of the floor, the little girl came whimpering up close to her mother. "Oh, Mama," she said. "It was so terrible, Mama—out there. It was so terrible when it tried to get me out there." The little girl threw herself against her mother and held tight to her, sobbing with relief.

"Out there?" the mother said.

But the little girl could not answer. How was it possible to speak anymore? Her insides hurt her so much with her fear.

"Hush, just hush," the mother said, with one hand holding the little girl's head against her chest while with the other hand steadily turning the crank that kept feeding more sheets through the rollers of the ancient wringer-washer she had.

"Now, now," the mother said. "You're right here with me now," the mother said, but her hand kept wheeling the crank around, so that more and more wet wash kept being squeezed through the angry rollers—and now, for the very first time in her life, the little girl understood what it was to be truly—hopelessly, irredeemably—afraid. **Q**

Under the Light

It was a bone-cracker for sure, the last fastball that caught her just below the elbow bone. Too bad she ducked. Too bad she turned her head and blinked. Too bad for her, Harry said, she didn't hang in there and catch it. If he and Tom had told her once, then they'd told her over a hundred billion times before to watch the ball and use the mitt, and not just only the mitt's middle part either, but the webbed part mostly, if ever anyway she wanted those purple welts of broken vessels in her hand to heal. No use, Harry said, for her to belly-ache and ask to pitch. She had had her chance and was strictly minor league. This was the majors. Sliders, curves, and knucklers, split-fingers and spitters—stuff she didn't have. If she wanted to play—and she was lucky, really, they let her play, Harry said—she had to catch. Too bad, he said, he was sorry, Harry told his mother, that she always, always, always bailed out, turned her head and blinked exactly when she oughtn't.

But, still, "Oh, man!" Harry said to Tom, "Did you hear that smack? I mean, like my dad's leather belt, that smack was. It was rocks against concrete! Take a look," Harry said, and lifted up his mother's glove-sided arm from off where it was lying limp against his mother's body lying on its side like to sleep, "Did you ever see a thing like this? Stitches? Stitches?" Harry said, touching his finger to where the ball's lacing had made an imprint on the slack-skinned place which was closer really, Harry noticed, a red and swelling stamp of cross-hatched baseball stitching, really closer to the more breakable part of his mother's blue-veined wrist than to her elbow.

Harry and Tom took a side each in heaving Harry's mother up from where she was down to finish off the full-count. Harry walked back and forth in front of his mother, holding his one arm slung low from the shoulder, showing her how to shake it out. Three balls and two strikes was the count, Harry was telling his mother, two outs, bottom of the ninth, bases loaded. No time for pain-complaining sissy-wristers. The game?—bottom of the ninth, 1963. No chokes! "One more man," he told her. "We've got to get this one last man!"

Harry's mother socked her fist into his father's mitt. She palm-jostled her crotch like a major leaguer. She rubbed spit into the stitched-in stamp above her wrist. She squatted onto her haunches and showed to Harry the sweet spot for the final strike.

What a sport!

What a mother!

Every pitch—bottom of the ninth, 1963!—every pitch always the last pitch! No chokes, no way! They were hot! They were on! Never did they not get their last man. Nearly every day of most of that summer they had lost some men but never at least in their game the last man. In the in-between evening and nighttime time of barbecue breezes searing over neighborhood fences there were windups and pitches and strikeouts that left Harry, his mother, and Tom the high-fiving champions of the backyard world they, the all of them, lived together in.

What else? Champagne is what else! What else but champagne! Champagne and orange juice for the champs! Mimosas, Harry's mother said, no more than two apiece for Harry and Tom, please, she said, Harry's mother popping off the cork top for Harry and Tom to fight to catch, Harry's mother next flopping down to soak whatever part of herself she had used that day instead of the mitt in the ice-chest the champagne all summer long chilled in, Harry's mother having soaked so far this summer her foot, her shin, her knee, her other foot, her cheek, and now today her elbow, or not her elbow but the still—even still!—lace-stamped place nearer to her wrist. T-bones, too, is what else! Harry aimed his nose at the side-neighbor's slump-stone wall and used a summer's worth of smelling to pick out burning beef from what tonight

was neither chicken, lamb, nor pork and began to chant
T-bone! T-bone! T-BONE! with Tom joining in and with
Harry's mother downing her mimosa and hauling herself up
and out to the garage and the meat-locker deep-freeze to fetch
her boys some sixteen-ouncers. Burgers and dogs, fries, chips,
and pickles, biting tomatoes like apples—and skip the chin-
napkins—rolling corn on the cob straight in the butter, eating
fancy olives one by one from off of each finger, nor either to
forget the nose-fuzzing mimosas, and the sweet things, too,
cakes, cookies, pies, and ice cream, home-made, hand-cranked
and rock-salted, June 11, July 19, August 28, none of them the
days of birthdays or holidays of anybody or of anything any of
them knew about or cared about except to celebrate the everyday that they were the champs, that they had got the one last
man, full-count, bases loaded, had struck him out, bottom of
the ninth, 1963!

Harry and Tom sat and sipped their mimosas, resting up
for the night game of what would mark their first double-
header, both of them waiting on the dark to try out the light,
each of them forearm-deep now in his own bag of the brand-
name, good kind of ridged-type dippers—no more jippo bargain chips for champs!

"What a life!" Harry said.

"Can you beat it?" Tom said.

"Sure you can beat it!" Harry said.

You could beat it with a real catcher, Harry said, who never
bailed out, one who you could throw as hard as you could at
and not have to feel bad about it after. Or good about it.
Because even though you could never tell it to your mother,
it did feel pretty good, Harry said, tagging her that way without
really having even to try too hard, and so much feeling good
over a mean thing like that could always make a person feel
pretty bad about himself. There was that for sure—the feeling
good when you ought to feel bad, the feeling bad at having felt
good—and then there was on top of it the bigger lie about the
bottom of the ninth and giving it all you had on every pitch like

it was the last pitch, because even though Harry had told his
mother he'd been giving it all he had to get the one last man,
he had not. Oh, he could throw a lot harder, Harry said to
Tom, said he guessed if he wanted to, said he could probably
break his mother's wrist if he really let loose and winged one
in there the way he knew he could if he only had a catcher who
would hang in there and catch it.

Harry watched Tom lean back on the lawnchair he was
sitting on and tip the chip bag to get out the last of the crumbs,
Tom saying "If, if, and if" into the bottomed-out hollow of the
rattling bag.

Harry licked the chip salt from off his fingers. He rinsed
his mouth out with mimosa and pinched a dip of snuff from the
chew can in his pocket. He loaded up his lower lip, spitting and
saying that he was just saying he could throw a lot harder is
all. Harry picked up his father's mitt his mother was using and
listened to Tom not believing Harry could throw any harder,
Tom asking Harry why would he anyway want to throw the ball
that hard at his mother anyhow? did Harry forget already
those welts of broken vessels in her hand? the baseball lacing
just this day imprinted into her wrist? not to say word one
about the places on her she often after the right number of
mimosas pulled down her pants and up her shirt to show to
Harry and Tom, who had to turn their heads to keep from
seeing either the prunes-in-cottage-cheese color of the bruises
in her flesh, or the newspaper yellow of her four-hook brassiere, and the sag of slickish underwear worn too big and sure
to shake a scare into the illusions of any growing boy who
looked too long. "Look at this!" she'd say. "And this!" she'd
say. "Did you ever believe a body could bruise so bad? I'm a
banana," Harry's mother would say, "a regular mush of tropi-
cal fruit. Make up your mother another mimosa, Harry," she'd
say, "and how about we play some cards now? How about a
few quick games of blackjack?" But Harry rarely let them play
cards but said instead that he was in training, a single-minded
baseball pitcher bent on more than backyard glory. "This is

the majors!" he'd say. "This is the All Stars, the World Series," he'd say, "this is the bottom of the ninth, 1963!" Harry
would say and say, getting them all to saying it themselves,
maybe even to believing it themselves, believing in the all-or-
nothing nature of the thing they did so strongly that Tom now
said it seemed more and more certain to him that Harry never
held back so much as a breath in the pitches that he threw, but
that he used his legs and back and skinny whip of arm to grind
his teeth and let it fly. And if that wasn't true, Tom said, and
if Harry really wanted to throw the way he said he knew he
could, then why didn't Harry let Tom catch? why didn't Harry
let Tom take the place behind the plate, hold up for Harry the
big target of Harry's father's major league mitt?

Harry slipped the chew can back into his back pocket on
the circle-worn side. He pincered open and shut the stiff-
leathered crawdad claw of his father's mitt. Harry spit out a
sluicing arc of tobacco juice any pine-riding minor leaguer
would envy, saying, "Why? Because she can't pitch and she
can't hit either is why! If she wants to play the game, she's got
to play by the rules is why! And besides all that, she likes it!"
Harry said, Harry saying to Tom, "Watch this!" and hollering
wise-guy style, shouting, "How you doing?" through the window screen to his mother he knew would now be microwave-
thawing out the frozen T-bones in the kitchen. "I said, how's
your elbow!" Harry shouted. "I mean, hey, your wrist! I mean,
suck it up, sport! Bottom of the ninth!" Harry shouted, taking
off his father's mitt and pulling up out of the ice-chest another
bottle of champagne, thumbing the cork to the critical point,
then shooting the cork thooping over the side-neighbor's
slump-stone wall.

"Bottom of the ninth!" said Harry's mother through the
kitchen screen. "T-bones coming up," she said. "What'll it be
tonight, men?" said Harry's mother, coming out with a platter
in each hand, and elbowing open the sliding glass door, asking
Harry to make his mother up another mimosa.

Harry made up his mother a mostly champagne mimosa,

champagne mostly because he thought he could see his mother thinking blackjack for the night, or poker or pinochle, or crazy eights, or go fish—any easy gamble to get herself out of having to catch the second game—any old card game Harry knew he and Tom could in short order clean Harry's mother out in if she got again to where she could not even see the deck that Harry was dealing from.

Harry's mother set the T-bones down to sizzle on the grill. Harry gave Tom the eye to let him know what was what, what it was being having to get Harry's mother past the place of the high-fiving champ and into the shoes of the champagne-headed celebrant without stopping off in the middle place, where she would get herself all long-faced and weepy-seeming, sad, a drag, no more sport, but an ordinary woman wanting always to talk about the problems in her past that Harry figured it was high time she passed out of. No more time for ordinary! If he and Tom had told her about how to use the webbed part of the mitt a hundred billion times, then they had warned her off her ass-dragging around the house about a hundred zillion times more than that! Nobody loves a loser. Nobody wants to hear it. And especially not Harry and Tom, who had already heard it just as many jillion times as they had told her not to tell it. Speed was the game! No time for talk! Put up or shut up! Play ball! Don't forget, bottom of the ninth, 1963!

Harry lifted up his plastic cup.

"Drink up!" Harry said. "Here's to us all!"

Just think of it—mimosas! T-bones! Coleslaw and the ridged-type dippers! A fresh can of chew and a brand new light for the night game of their first doubleheader! So close, so close!

It was too good to look at and too good not to see, the only hard part in any of it being hoping your mother did not drink too much, but hoping still she didn't drink too little. It was rounding third base and getting the no-slide signal, taking the final coasting turn for home to make a standup score. It was

Harry hearing already his mother skip over her ass-dragging past, Harry's mother moving herself straight into the here-and-now and onto Harry, going at him again about the staining dangers of tobacco, pulling down her lower lip to show to Harry her teeth and gums, Harry's mother saying to Harry how the tobacco would discolor everything, rot, even. "You want your teeth to fall out?" she wanted to know. "Look at my wrist," said Harry's mother. "Can you see this? You want your gums to be the color of my wrist? Or of my leg?" said Harry's mother. "Hey, did I show you my leg?" she said.

"No," said Harry. "You didn't show me your leg. You'd better just keep that leg to yourself," Harry said. "And if you really want me to see your wrist," he said, "then I'll have to turn the light on. Otherwise," said Harry, "what you ought to do is soak that wrist until after we all eat."

But they did not the all of them eat. Tom ate. Harry ate. But Harry's mother did not eat, Harry's mother being taken lately to saying she was watching her figure by means of a liquid diet she said it was helping her to lose to be on. So she drank. It was fine so far as the cards went on the nights when she drank, but somewhere in the middle of her fourth, fifth, or sixth mimosa it came to Harry's head the idea his mother might not keep herself in any kind of shape to take her place behind the plate. It came to Harry's head the idea that maybe he and Tom ought not to have eaten the meaty halves of her T-bone the way that she had told them to do, leaving her to gnaw the skimpy part where she assured them the meat was always sweeter next to. "Really," she said, "this is all I need. You boys eat. Eat," she said. "There's plenty," she said. "Plenty more where this came from."

Harry put his mitt on. He ate his ice cream from his mitt, holding the bowl deep in the pocket. He watched Tom eating his ice cream the same way, and watched his mother keeping on her liquid diet, cutting out now the orange-juice part without this time even blaming it on what she called the acidic condition of her stomach. Harry heard Tom start in to scraping his spoon against his bowl, a sound sadder to Harry than the emptiest bag of the best ridged dippers. Harry saw his mother unwinding the wires from around the top of another champagne bottle. Harry and Tom looked first one at the other and then back at Harry's mother, who was aiming the bottle off in the direction of the side-neighbor's slump-stone wall, thumbing the cork and shooting it off over to where she had always told Harry and Tom to please stop shooting them, the cork disappearing out into the darkness Harry could no longer see through. His mother filled herself up. Harry picked up the baseball and began to snap the ball into his mitt where the finished-up ice-cream bowl wasn't anymore.

What they had going here was not a full-count. This was not two outs, bottom of the ninth, bases loaded. There was no last pitch here. There was no last man. This was not the bottom of the ninth, 1963. What they had going here was a momentum stopper, a rally killer, what was occurring to Harry as the sudden buggish itching so much silence in his mother gave him.

Harry said, "Don't you want to play some cards?"

"No," said Harry's mother. "No, I think I better rest."

"That's right," said Tom. "You better rest."

"Rest?" Harry said. "That's it? Rest?"

"Rest," said Harry's mother. "For the next game," she said.

"All right," Harry said. "Good, then, you just rest. Ice your wrist, why don't you? I think I'll turn on the light."

"Can you wait?" Harry's mother said. "Let me finish resting? Can you wait a little while? Give me ten more minutes?"

Harry bumped his thumb along the baseball's raised-up stitching. He smacked the ball against the cement porch. He caught the ball off the rebound, and said he guessed he didn't see right off why not he couldn't wait another ten more minutes. Harry watched his mother put her champagne cup into the big league pocket of his father's mitt to have another mimosa out of from. Tom stuck out his mitt, too, and wondered whether he might have another along with Harry's mother so long as all they were doing was resting.

It was the kind of a thing you had to see it to believe it, Harry's mother needing not to play a game of cards to keep from playing ball, needing not to fill the quiet times of the night with all the used-up words she'd thrown out all of those hundred billion times before. Harry leaned back on his lawn-chair to look up at the blank sky blackening above him. He tapped his mitt against his leg, trying to figure back to how many heartbeats ago it was when waiting was easy.

Another ten more minutes!

How many seconds in another ten more minutes? Ten times sixty seconds is how many! Six hundred seconds! You just tap your mitt against your leg another six hundred more times, Harry, and we'll be ready! You just let us rest until you can count the first six hundred stars to come out tonight and we'll play ball. Give us another six hundred swallows and we'll be primed for the night game of this here backyard double-header.

Harry reloaded up his lower lip. He arced a perfect spitter out onto the lawn and muscled up his tongue for the locker-room lashing he could see his team was in sore need of. Then he stood up from out of the lawn chair and started in to pacing the cement porch, socking now his fist, now the baseball into his mitt, beginning by saying to his mother and Tom that never to Harry's knowing had there ever been a single Hall of Famer made famous on the strength of waiting and resting. Never had Harry heard of a time where the winner said he owed his crown to a blood-rare slab of T-bone meat and another ten more minutes to digest it in peace. Imagine it! Imagine, Harry said, the one last man waiting while you rested in the dark, slamming down the champagne, digesting the food to fuel the next last pitch you expected to strike him out again with, asking the one last man to please wait, to sit still awhile, to let you rest a bit before you caught him flat-footed with the final strike. "Fat chance!" he said. "This isn't little league! This isn't the minors! This is the big leagues, the majors!" Harry said, "the bottom of the ninth, 1963!" he said.

So what did Tom say?

"See what your mother says," said Tom.

And what did Harry's mother say?

"It's hard, Harry," said Harry's mother. "I'm tired. It's hard, honey," she said, "playing two games."

So who ever said it would be easy?

Listen, what did you have to do with a mother like this!

What you had to do for openers was you had to leave your best friend and only mother sitting soft-headed from too much champagne drunk in the dark to start yourself to throwing against your side-neighbor's slump-stone wall. You had to start off like to finish, throwing from the get-go the kind of wall-chippers that when the other guy heard cracking off the slump-stone he got too scared to take the bat in hand to face you. What you had to do was to keep on playing hard until the other guy dropped, then keep on playing harder. You had to convince yourself. You had to knock a wall down. You needed to be able each time to reach back and throw the high, hard one and hit the mark on the slump-stone wall that would send the ball right back to where you wanted it to go so as to pick it up and do it again. You had to work the hitch out from your windup, perfect the rhythm of your stride. You did it with your eyes closed. You did it in the dark. You had to learn to live inside yourself in a world where there was no time to wake up what might have died inside you. You had already to be in a sweat. You needed to show to Tom and to your mother the only reason to fill up the way they did was to burn it all off in the playing of the next game, and then the next, until the last game had been played out and was in the record books for good and all.

But what Harry missed seeing in six hundred seconds of slump-stone wall-bashing, and what he saw when Tom called him over was not Tom and his mother with mitts on and making ready to take the field for the second game, but Harry's

mother and Tom still laid up in the locker room, three-quar-
ters crocked on the lawnchair benches, sunk deeper than ever
into a post-champagne disarray, his mother not saying anything or even making a twitch of a move to raise her head up
from where it was buried down deep between her knees.

"I think she's sick," said Tom.

"Sick?" said Harry.

"Said she's feeling sort of puny."

"Puny?"

"Puny," Tom said, Tom standing what Harry guessed
Tom must have thought to be a good safe distance from
Harry's mother to wait and watch and see what next.

"The light," said Harry. "What we need here is a little
light."

Harry saw his mother lift her head to squint against the
light and see him standing at the switch, and it didn't look
good, the little bit of her what Harry saw before his mother's
head dropped back down between her knees. Harry circled
around his mother to approach her from behind, and with his
pitching hand he gathered together a fistful of her hair, while
with his glove hand he lifted her up by her listless shoulder.
Harry's mother's jaw fell down when her head came up, and
the dim-wittedest bat-boy could have seen that the problem
was not entirely too much champagne but had probably more
exactly to do with the specks of chewing tobacco he saw stuck
all on her teeth.

"You gave her a chew?" Harry said.

"She said she wanted one," said Tom. "She said she
wanted to spit like we did."

Harry turned his mother's head toward himself. It seemed
to him that her skin was getting to be a sort of a cadaverous
color by the light of the light that Harry began to see would
not this night be used for the second game of the double-
header they had planned to play, Harry's mother saying now
that yes, she didn't guess she felt so good. Could Harry help
her to the toilet? Could he help his mother to her feet?

Harry helped his mother, noticing as he hoisted her up, his mother's wrist, the only living color on her body that he could see, her wrist still—how many hours now?—showing the cross-hatched stitching red in the center of a patch of purple swollen almost to the size of the baseball Harry had thrown to make it that way.

"I think its broken, dear," Harry's mother said.

"I don't think so," Harry said.

"Might be," Tom said.

"Maybe a chip," Harry said. "But not a break."

"It's broken, dear," Harry's mother said. She said, "Hurry."

They made it to the toilet, Harry and his mother, with Tom tagging along to make sure, Tom saying it sounded to him like there was some serious porcelain prayer going on inside there, some major league heaving for sure. Lucky for her, Tom was saying, she hadn't eaten the way he and Harry had. "Could you imagine it," Tom wanted to know, "a T-bone coming up? Or how about those chips?" Tom said. "Double lucky for her she didn't eat any of those ridged dippers," he said. But even still with the luck and all, Tom supposed it was a rookie move, Harry's mother getting sick like that from off of only the half-pinch of tobacco that he had given to her.

"Your's was the rookie move," Harry said, Harry saying to Tom that Tom had done exactly what Harry's mother had wanted him to do. "She's a veteran," Harry said. "She got you soft. She got you to sitting in the dark with women. Did she tell you one game was enough?" Harry said. "Did she tell you you couldn't do it all? That you had to make a choice? Listen up," Harry said to Tom. "Champions never choose."

Harry put his ear against the door to hear his mother finishing up losing the rest of what she didn't have to lose.

"Are you all right?" Harry asked his mother. "Are you drowning in there?"

"No," said Harry's mother. "No, I'm not drowning. I'm getting my second wind. I'm getting ready for this second game. I'm brushing my teeth. Are you ready?" she said. "How's your arm?" she said.

Her second wind!

Could you beat it? Could you beat the Babe, the Mick, Maris, or Mays? She was coming out from the toilet to play the second game! And this, try beating this—try topping the picture of Harry's mother, coming out of the bathroom like to take the field after only the seventh-inning stretch, taking, too, a fast hold of Harry's ear to drag him along and tell him that if he wanted to see a champion to come on out and try her. Top Harry hung up by his ear, top him tiptoed and never for an instant trying to pull out from his mother's grip, Harry remembering in her pinch of calloused finger-pads how strong this woman who filled out a four-hook brassiere could really be.

Who here was the champ? Who here didn't have what it took to take the bat in hand? Just ask Tom, who was telling Harry he'd just as soon sit it out on the lawnchair bench for this one, Harry's mother telling Harry not even should he think about sitting it out, telling him to shut up his mouth and pick up his mitt to start this night game she was sick of hearing how much he had been saying he wanted to play so bad. "Come on!" she said. "Bottom of the ninth!" Harry's mother said. "Let's play ball, Drake!"

Here it was! Here they were! The classic match-up! Here was Harry on the mound, there his mother behind the plate, the both of them alone and under the light at last!

Harry kicked his cleat against the rubber. He squeezed the ball inside his mitt. He passed his arm across his forehead and stared down at his mother squatted out there on her haunches. Harry could taste it in his arm, the blood-rare flavor of red meat, as he studied the target his mother held up for him to throw at, Harry set already to shake off the signals he expected his mother to give him. No chance of this night throwing anything like a change-of-pace—no, he would stick with the heat, throwing fastballs to show to Tom, to show to her, what smoke could look like, what real fire could sound like when it left Harry's hand and blazed a straight line through the night to split the plate, a leathered splat in his father's big league mitt, the sound of the champion nailing down the one last man.

But never did Harry see his mother signal for a single change-of-pace, but he heard her holler instead for him to throw still harder, Harry beginning to turn loose now the kind of slump-stone wall-chippers he could not believe he was really throwing, could not believe his mother would really have the stuff to catch.

His mother did not bail out. She did not blink. Nor did she quit with her chatter—but called out to Harry that he would never get the one last man if what he had thrown so far was the best he had. "Bush league!" she shouted. "Rag arm!" she screamed. She didn't even need a mitt, she said, to catch his limp-wristed pitches. "It's gone!" she said. "Over the wall, out of the park!" she yelled—and she did it, in a single easy motion Harry saw her do it, saw his mother throw his father's mitt up and over onto the dark side of the slump-stone wall Harry had all summer tried to throw through.

Harry took his time. He worked the ball in his hand, trying to find the right killer grip for the next last pitch he found he could not throw, Harry feeling in each of the raised-up stitches the first mark to be struck in his big league record under the column for losses. He saw his mother waving and clapping her bare-skinned hands, saw his mother rock down now from her haunches to her knees, Harry's mother asking him what was wrong, why didn't he throw, what was the matter, couldn't he see, couldn't he see her?

"Can't you see?" she said. "Hey, Drake! Can't you see me?" his mother said. "Come on, baby, burn it in here! Show us what you've got! Let's get this lousy man! Come on, can you see me, champ? Come on," she said. "You know you can see me. I'm here, baby—here's your mother, sonny boy!" **Q**

JOHN LOWRY

Captions

He spent a fortune trying to remove every blemish from her ass. Just before orgasm, her face became grave. Try to think of existence as another form of television. When I'm alone with the cat, the two of us sit looking at the door. For him, life was a slow leak in the engine room. He always waited for her breasts to touch the eggs. When she died, a portion of North America grew quieter. Sundays at home put an end to his greatness. She always limped after they had quarreled. She loved the nights he turned criminal. She said, Soon, if you don't mind, I will take a bite of you. His talk of greatness made me think of peas falling into a pot. A fly must feel that he is constantly doing something wrong. I've always wanted to organize the crumbs. He made love as though poring over a map. In Cincinnati, she reasoned, the men were broken-hearted. **Q**

Overpopulation

I got up at daybreak, had coffee, and drove to the office. My secretary was already hard at work. She brought me my mail, faxes, and a second cup of coffee. My in-box was full. The phones were ringing. Messages were piling up. Another busy day.

After eleven, I buzzed Martha. I would be back after lunch, I said. I took the stairs to the basement and got on the elevator marked South. It only took a few seconds. When the doors opened, the light was blinding, the heat like a furnace. My locker was against the far wall. I opened it and replaced my L.A. suit with a flowered shirt, a ruana, and a sombrero. I looked out at the square. The dust threw up a haze of light. A dog trotted by, every rib showing. A bus lurched up a side street, belching smoke, people sitting on the roof, hanging on to its sides.

My partner was at our stand, turning a few more pots. We nodded and I squatted next to her. I began to sweat. It was like sitting inside an explosion. A farmer came through the square leading a donkey pulling a cart topped up with dung. A woman followed, wrapped like an Arab, holding a baby. A tourist bus pulled up. A bunch of Taiwanese got off, looked around, and got back on again. Two young men came over to us. They had a camcorder. One of them took pictures while the other pointed to our pottery.

"How much? *Combien*? *Cuanto*?"

My partner pointed to our little sign. The young man got angry. Too much. We were trying to cheat them because they were tourists. They were smarter than that.

"What's exciting here?" the one with the camcorder said.

"The bullfights on Sunday," I said.

He looked at his watch.

"Today's Wednesday."

They walked back to the bus and it went away.

My partner lay down on her mat. Siesta, she said with a smile. I nodded and lit up some of the marijuana she kept under the stand. A breeze came up, raising sheets of dust, and died away. Two guys came into the square. They had big mustaches and kind of ambled, their hands in their back pockets. I saw them look over at me. I pretended to be asleep. When they walked off, I woke my partner and told her about the men. I pointed to my watch.

"Ah, Uncle Sam," she said.

I went back to the elevator, changed my clothes, and pressed the button. Nothing happened. The light was on, but nothing happened. I looked at my watch. I had a meeting in ten minutes. The two guys walked by again, stopping to look at me in my gringo clothes. I banged the button. I held it down with my fist. Minutes went by.

"This is ridiculous!" I shouted. "This is the U.S.A. I demand an elevator!" **Q**

Straight

They had all come back to do what they had not already done. For instance, the bully was there. He was trying to handcuff me to my bed. He wanted me to sing. He said, "Sing!"

Mom was pouring iced tea, emptying ashtrays, putting her hands on their arms and their shoulders. They'd got her shirt off. They were taking turns standing behind her and putting their hands on her brassiere. They were sticking their hands in her hair. They were pushing my mom in different places.

"Sing an area," the bully said to me.

He said *area.*

Some of them had their cocks out. But I was trying to watch out for my mom.

Mom said, "Call the police! Get out of here! Go get the neighbors!"

One of the men was naked and he was beating off and screaming, "You think this risible?"

There was a blanket over my mom and over the man who was on top of her on the couch. My mom yelled, "Somebody massage my feet!"

"Mom," I said. "Telephone," I said. "I can't concentrate," I said. "Be careful, Mom," I said.

"Just do some scales or something," the bully said.

I touched his arm. I squeezed it. I sipped my iced tea.

"You don't understand," I said.

I saw Mom sitting on a chair. "Jesus," I heard her say. I saw her freshen up her hair with her fingertips. I saw her smooth out her eyebrows—get them wet to get the little hairs to all lie down straight.

Ah, sweet mystery of life, at last I've found thee. . . . **Q**

Love

Younger guy reaches to turn switch on machine to *off*, keep smoke from cigarette out of eyes, look out window. Other guy moves things around, puts the big things in different places, reorders the room. Machine far from chair; younger guy stretches to reach. Other guy pulls chair across room— wood chair across wood floor. Younger guy sits on floor, gets ashtray, gets book. Younger guy sits yoga style. Younger guy says, "Everything's about war with you."

Other guy laughs. Walks to machine, past younger guy. Turns switch on machine to *on*. He leaves. Slams door.

Younger guy laughs. Turns switch on machine to *off*. **Q**

On the Street

The mother had told the boy that he need not stay awake, but the boy had made up his mind to stay awake. The man was also awake. He had a beard, and wore a flannel shirt. The floor was hardwood, and the man and the mother were standing on it. The boy touched his hand to the cloth on the sofa. All of the windows were open, and the boy could feel a wind coming in. The boy had seen the mother shaking, but the mother had said to the boy that she was not afraid. The boy was wearing his pajamas. The mother said one thing loudly enough for the boy to hear: "George." The boy had three animals, in a cage, in his room, not just dead, but cut into pieces and placed throughout the cage. The mother had said she was tired of it. The boy had heard cat sounds from the TV while he was in his bed, when his bed had been at the man's house. The man had said that he, the man, was angry, and he had thrown a book onto the floor. The boy fell asleep. The mother's green car was parked outside, on the street.

It went on past midnight.

The man smoked a cigarette.

The mother boiled water. **Q**

Fatigues

I just fell asleep in Temy's bed one time and slept right there all night long. My papa never lets me sleep in his bed.

My papa says, *Give me a good workout.* But all he wants is me rubbing his big stomach. He turns over and says, *Yeah, right there.* His back, okay, I do not mind rubbing his back. And his legs, I know he has to stand all day on his legs. But I do not see how he tires out his stomach that it needs so much rubbing.

That's it, he says, *right there.*

Me and Temy played pool this one time at a bar. He broke, and Temy has a good clean break and he made the balls go all over that table, clear down to where his white ball was to start with. Well, I was stripes, and I played a good game. Temy sunk the white ball with the eight ball, so he lost. But I maybe could have won anyway.

I'd say I maybe could have.

All me and my papa play is checkers. I am black, he is red. We don't talk. He just looks at the board and thinks of how to take my checkers. My papa's big. But he is not stupid. He can play checkers, and checkers, he says, is a thinker's game.

After we play checkers, we play Truth or Dare. Except we only dare. We never do Truth.

My papa was in a war. He still has these green-and-brown pants that he likes to see me wear. He says me wearing those pants reminds him of the war. He says I look good in those pants. He says I am his boy, wearing my papa's war pants.

· · ·

I got to breathing so fast I felt dizzy, and my feet up in the air like they were, one foot got this bad cramp halfway through, that night I slept over at Temy's. But I paid no mind to that cramped-up foot—I just let Temy keep going. Just breathing and breathing and waiting for Temy to finish so that Temy will know that I will do whatever he wants me to do, so Temy will know that I am his boy.

The only way I let my papa do it to me is me on my knees, leaning down on my elbows. And I make sure he uses a lot of lotion, and I make him go slow, at least to start. Not that his thing is so big—but with Papa, I have to get relaxed, and it takes me some time to get relaxed.

After, I just lay there facedown on the bed. Papa goes and gets a towel, cleans me up, himself too. Then he says, *Run along to sleep now.* But Papa won't lay down until I'm gone. He sits on the side of the bed and waits for me to leave. My papa just has his special ways.

I keep having this dream while I am sleeping. I do not know what it could mean.

I saw a picture of my papa when he was young. He was outside with a dog. Papa has on short pants and no shoes. He is not fat in this picture. He is down with his dog, talking to it, or maybe he is kissing it. Anyway, Papa has his hands around the dog, holding it.

I do not know if Temy wanted me sleeping in his bed all night or if he just fell asleep and forgot. I could not sleep for a while, wondering.

I thought I had done good, let him finish, stayed quiet. I did not say what I wanted to say, which was, *I'm sorry, I have to go, Temy. Get off! Let me get up! I have to go home!* Q

Here in America

Her hair was cut so high you could see where her ears ended, their very tips, delicate and veiny. I ran my lips where it had been snipped away. Her skirt also ended quickly, until my hands, disoriented in the dark, weren't sure where they were, what they were touching. I imagined I was swimming through her, stretched out until my feet hooked over the bottom of the bed.

"No, seriously," she said, still chatting in a cocktail-party way. "In Berlin I can go anywhere, at any hour, and there is always fun, and there is always friends."

"That's because Europe is an ant colony," I grunted.

I was looking for the right place to put my mouth. But it was so dark, like an air raid we were sitting out in each other's body.

"A what?"

"Ant colony. Everyone's the same. Here in America—"

And then we found each other. I couldn't tell before if she'd been struggling or helping. Now I heard her mutter or sigh one long syllable that sounded almost Japanese.

"So-o-o . . ."

She was a professional, who would be on top, so I could watch the beginning of her second chin, where the tiny residue of what her face had seen was collecting, a pouch, just its shadow, shaking slightly each time she rose and fell. Then she would walk away. That was part of it. I would watch her body, her spine, the cleft of her ass, then each leg, utterly natural and animal, on her way to the kitchenette to get coffee.

"Why do guys like it that way?" she asked.

"What way?"

"Like this."

She put my penis between her breasts.

"*I* don't like it that way," I said, looking up as far as I could from where I lay, frowning.

". . . weird of them," she went on, bouncing, maneuvering on the mattress, which was just a fold-out sofa. The smell of old, nicotine-infested cushions and bolsters was all around us.

Of course, she wasn't really German. That was an act. Everyone at the bar thought she was. "Beautiful Barla." It was to give her an excuse for being there, that she was a foreign student and didn't have a green card and studied film at NYU. That's what she told guys, so they wouldn't think she was a whore. "I am just, how do you say? A bar girl."

That first night, before I knew, I asked her all about Germany, nervous that she wasn't asking me to leave, that she was smoking cigarettes and putting them out in an old ice-cream dish by the side of the bed.

"Yes, in some ways it is better. But of course you don't have the *freedom* there."

"I want to owe you," I said. "I mean, I want to *pay* you."

"We can make this a regular thing, yes?"

And that's how it began. She dropped the accent later on, when we got to know each other. At least I'm paying my way, I told myself. That made me feel better. I got to watch her from underneath, with total removal, as if I were an anatomist. And when I went to the club again and asked for her, they said she didn't work there anymore. So she'd found another source of income.

Me.

I spent hours staring at her forehead. It was perfectly empty and depthless, like the marble of a statue.

"How is it," I'd ask, "that your face is so smooth and clear?"

I looked all through her cosmetics in the bathroom, for what I don't know. Some magic cream that explained how she could move me so much, yet be unreal at the same time, just a paid girl. I watched myself from the corner of the room, her walking away, climbing up onto the bed, climbing up on top of me. The same motion.

"This is an almost dreamlike state you're describing," the psychiatrist said.

"Yeah. It's instead of dreaming, I go to her. I don't dream."

"Everyone dreams," he said. "You just don't remember your dreams."

"Same thing."

He was confined to a wheelchair. Not that he was in it. He was in a nice, comfortable armchair when I came in. The door had been open. But I glimpsed the wheelchair as I passed the little kitchen. And I noticed he never got up. The phone was on a side table. I sat across from him.

"I walk out the door. And I lock it behind me. And I turn around. And there's nowhere I want to go. I just stand out in the hallway. Then I turn around and go back in."

"You're depressed," he said.

"So how do I get undepressed?"

"It takes a long time."

". . . and a lot of money."

But he was putting on his glasses. His hands were big and bony on his starved wrists. What did he have? I wondered. He wrote me a few numbers and names.

"Unfortunately, I'm not taking any new patients. These are some doctors I can recommend."

It was a nice apartment, with bric-a-brac and greenery all over the place. I didn't think you were supposed to see where people like this lived. It was the first time I'd ever been to one. There was that kind of old, thick, white lead paint, like frosting, on all the doors and window frames.

"But I like you. Couldn't you see me a few more times?"

His glasses were on the end of his nose. He smiled.

"You like my apartment?"

"Yes."

His hands were pressing against the arms of the chair, as if he were trying to get up, but he wasn't, he was just rigid all of a sudden.

"You okay?"

"Not yet," he said, to someone above me, or over my shoulder.

Then, whatever it was passed, and he sat back, looking past me, out the window at the building opposite.

"I wonder if you'd mind phoning someone?"

"One of these guys?" I held up the sheet of notepaper he'd given me.

"No," he said. "A real doctor."

I didn't get in touch with anyone else. I knew who I wanted.

"I *can't* see you professionally," he said over the phone.

"Well, then how about unprofessionally? I won't pay you. I mean, I'll pay you in some other way. I'll help around the house."

"I have people to do that, thanks."

"What have you *got,* anyway?"

"A bad cold at the moment. Good-bye."

I found myself walking the streets all night, ending up downtown at dawn, dancing almost, picking my way over the cobblestones, trying to stay on top of these giant molars, and realized I was drunkenly weaving, inviting violence. But nobody stopped me. I felt the mist rushing off the stone landscape. That rare sense of being on the sea.

"You ever had sex in front of the TV?"

"No."

She sat facing me on propped knees.

"Isn't this going to be hard for you?" I asked, trying to politely look over her shoulder.

"How much was she asking?"

"Who?"

"That other girl. Darlene."

"How do you know her name was Darlene?"

"From where you met her. From what she said."

"I thought you never did that. On the street, I mean."

"I'm writing a book," she said. That was her standard answer whenever I wondered why she knew certain things. "Lean back."

It was a deep wicker chair. It creaked with both our weights.

"Darlene's a man," she said.

It didn't work too well, logistics-wise, but she was right, it was incredibly erotic. When I got up, I felt the imprint of wicker all over my back.

"McDonald's." She picked up one of the bags. "This is terrible for you, this food."

"That's why I eat it."

After she left, I went to the closet, flipped out the belly of the old vacuum cleaner, and got more bills. I stuck a hundred in my back pocket and went out, leaving the TV on like a watchdog.

"Darlene?" I asked into the night.

There was nobody on the corner.

"Darlene?"

But she or he had either quit for the night or picked someone up.

I turned in a slow circle, letting chance choose my direction.

"Darlene?" **Q**

Responsibleman

They put him in charge of making sure nothing bad happened.

It happened.

"I accept full responsibility," he said.

"Don't worry," they said. "There was nothing you could do about it. Really."

"Still," he said. A boy and a girl had been run over by a train in Arkansas. "They were practically children," he said.

"Don't worry about it," they said.

"It won't happen again," Responsibleman said.

Would it happen again? Could it? He kept going over it in his mind: I didn't fall asleep. I didn't leave the door unlocked. I didn't leave the oven on.

How could it have happened?

It happened.

"My fault," he said.

"It was one of those things," they said. "There was nothing anyone could have done about it. We're giving you a raise."

"No," he said.

"You're doing a good job. You're the best man we've got. You're the most responsible person there is."

"Still," he said. He pointed to the newspaper clipping and shook his head. The headline said: "Building collapses in Tokyo."

"It happened in another part of the world," they said.

"But it happened," he said, "and I am to blame. Me," he said.

Everyone else looked at one another. They said, "Surely this man is Responsibleman."

Responsibleman heard them. "I can't help it," he said. **Q**

The Magic Bike

Kevin didn't know how to fix the broken one, so he decided he'd buy her a new one.

Her name was Lisa.

The guy at the bike shop, his name was Pete.

"I want to buy a bike," Kevin said.

The guy held out his hand to Kevin. "Pete," the guy said.

"Hi," said Kevin. "I want to buy a bike."

"What's your name?" Pete said.

"Kevin," Kevin said.

"Kevin," Pete said. "So you want to buy a bike, huh?" He scratched his head and looked around the shop. "I work here," he said, "but I don't own the place. The owner's on vacation in Texas or something. His name's Bob. Do you want a free T-shirt?"

"Okay," Kevin said.

Pete gave him a T-shirt. It said "Bicycle Bob's" on it. There was a picture of a bike. "I'll give you a good deal on a bike," Pete said. "Like I said, Kevin, the boss is out of town."

"Okay," Kevin said.

"How about this one?" Pete said. "It's fifty-five dollars."

The bike was blue and nice. It was an old three-speed with shiny fenders.

"Tell you what," Pete said, "I'll give it to you for free. You've been a good customer. We've got a million bikes and you probably don't have any."

Pete put air in the tires. "If anything goes wrong," Pete said, "just bring it back in and I'll fix you right up. You get a thirty-day guarantee, technically, but who's counting? Want another T-shirt?"

"That's okay," Kevin said.

"Here's one for your girl friend," Pete said. "All we got is large. I don't know how big she is."

"Thanks," Kevin said.

"No problem," Pete said.

He looked around the place. "Let's go have some coffee," Pete said.

"No, thanks," Kevin said.

"No problem," Pete said.

Kevin was driving home. The new bike was in the back seat of the car and the two Bicycle Bob's T-shirts were on the front seat with Kevin. Kevin stopped the car and got out. He put both T-shirts on, got the bike out, and rode it twenty miles to Lisa's house.

"I got you a bike," Kevin said.

Lisa cried.

They didn't have a car anymore, but they started finding money every time they went to the laundromat. **Q**

Hops

Coin's daughter Nadine takes Coin's free hand and tells Coin about the world. The world has a dry voice. She makes her voice dry, and she says her name.

Nadine is twenty-three.

Coin says her name, and he keeps her hand in his.

"Hops," she says. "Call me Hops."

Hops is a stuffed frog Coin bought Nadine years ago. Nadine wore it out and has tied a red bandana around its neck to keep its froggy head from sitting in its froggy lap. Hops is two shades of avocado and has a cloak-and-dagger grin.

Nadine and Coin are circling a pond in the Sculpture Garden at the Museum of Modern Art. She has always walked as if every step she takes is the first step she has ever taken. There is something wacky about Nadine's feet and odd in the set of her arms. She stops and admires a weighty sculpture, a ponderous Henry Moore. She swings Coin's hand. She says, "The world acts good-hearted. The world comes by and says hello. At parties, the world takes you aside. It has gotten you a drink. It lends you its tapes. You bring the world home, and it sits on your couch where it crosses its legs at the knee."

Nadine's sorrow is the sorrow of birds.

She is wearing a fifteen-hundred-dollar plum-colored cloth coat. Her skirt is black, and her shoes are tobacco brown. They're hightops. They have eyelets. White lace rises from each shoe and circles her ankles like doll collars. On her black sweater, where her heart is, she has pinned a red enamel heart.

Nadine's hand brings their hands up, and she holds them to Coin's chin. She tests Coin's grip. She says, "Arm wrestle?" She has her mother's mouth and her mother's eyes, her mother's ears. Where does Coin fit in?

Nadine drops his hand. She shifts a black iron chair and sits down, saying, "Your baby is having a baby, and I don't want it."

Coin tries to find the sky. What he sees is blue and firm. He bumps Picasso's *She-Goat.*

His heart's in his mouth.

Nadine is married to Coin's friend Michael. Michael is forty-two and has two ex-wives and five children. He and Coin own a restaurant they run.

Nadine says, "I always sit like this now." Her coat is open, and her knees show. She says, "Like I'm about to stand." She goes into her pocket and comes up with a cigar. There in her hand, it surprises her. She says, "Coin, a fine cigar." She holds it up like a scientist.

She offers it to Coin, saying, "It's yours. Have it. It's a find." She hunts in her pocket for what it was she was after and finds a deck of cards. She says, "Rook." On the box, a rook holds a hand it's been dealt.

Coin says, "Tennessee for Two." He is trying to unwrap the cigar.

Nadine says, "Kentucky Discard. Do you pass? I pass. Little Sweep and Big Sweep. My bid?" She opens the Rook box and says, "Few people know Rook, Coin. I sit close to strangers in the depot, on park benches, and I talk them into games. Teach me, they say. I have to."

Coin gives up on the cigar.

She says, "Play? You and me, one game for the championship of the world."

"No time," Coin says, and he buries the cigar in his overcoat. He helps her up, steadies her in front of him, and says, "Why are we here?"

She says, "Does Michael need six children?" She takes big steps around Picasso's *She-Goat,* in sunlight, her arms crossed high on her chest, her hands on her own shoulders.

When was it they had said all it was they were going to say to each other?

Outside, near her subway stop, Coin buys Nadine rum balls, and she has the sack open before he's paid.

He says, "Nadine." He says, "May I call you Nadine?"

"Hops," she says. "Hops has character. Hops tells you something."

Coin's heart skids and bangs around. It's a one-man band in his chest.

Nadine says, "I don't want anything to do with babies." She rolls a rum ball into her mouth and says, "Babies. Yuck." She wiggles her sticky fingers near Coin's face, teasing him and looking for help.

He gives her a handkerchief.

She says, "Coin, you need your beard. You wore it like an explosion." She makes bomb noises.

Coin cups his hands to his mouth and spreads them as if he is calling for help.

The story Michael tells is he was raised by wolves, not in some folktale way, but in real life. His hair is always knocked back in some kind of wet geometry. His eyes are negligent, and his beard is a dog's beard. He's got the Vietnam War under his belt, which he came home from, and then sold options twenty-four hours a day until he got rich.

Mornings he's down on Amsterdam Avenue in pickup basketball games. His hook's his ticket. It's an urgent wounded thing that can't be stopped.

Whenever Nadine is where Michael is she comes up like she's going to stand on his feet, and she puts her face in his face and talks his beard off.

Michael, at the bar, is gnawing on a pencil and looking at a woman when Coin comes in. She's across the room at a table. Michael'd like to be doing a cigarette ad. The woman is reading a box, turning it over and over, slowly, as if it is a light bulb that has burned out. It's noon, and she is dressed for night. Her high heels sit like crows on the floor. Coin picks up a sandwich and asks for coffee. He and Michael move to a table three feet away from the woman. Michael says, "Hello," and the woman studies her box. Michael says to Coin, "Her teeth."

The woman has put the box down, and is treating her hair violently. She's wrecking it.

Michael says, "One word, Coin." He taps his pencil against his teeth. "For white. For the white of her teeth. One word."

The box sits on the woman's table, and she bangs a fist down on each side of it. Her hair looks like a weedy hillside, like a van Gogh. She looks as if she is mad enough to eat the box.

Michael tucks his head under and pulls his feet off the ground. They pedal, bobbing and weaving, urgent. He's a man too big for the tricycle he's on. He says, "Pearls. Virginal."

Coin unwraps the pickles he's brought, then thumps his tie where his heart is, saying, "Pit-a-pat. Pit-a-pat. True love." He taps his heart, says, "Pit-a-pat."

Michael says, "Save me, Coin. Help." His head's down, and his feet have stopped. He's left with a foot on a foot.

Coin says, "Ivory. Snow-capped. Alabaster."

Michael eyes are hasty BB's. His feet are flatirons.

Coin says, "Lilies."

The woman lifts the box, only her fingertips touching it, and she undoes the lid, pulls up and out four tiny white triangles and removes a porcelain bird.

A tall woman, talking fast, comes in and sits at the woman's table. She is saying, "Paul Anka is alive and performing tonight." The woman Michael has been eyeing hands the tall woman the box, but keeps the bird. It's a robin. The tall woman takes the bird. She says, "God, don't you love it. Paul Anka. Alive." She can't fit the bird in the box. She says, "Didn't you think he was dead? Shot in Reno." She turns the robin over and searches its face, says to the bird, "You look swell."

Michael scoots his chair over. He is saying something about Paul Anka. He says, "Paul Anka is appearing. Like God."

Coin calculates what it would take to fall. If he tipped his chair this way or that, at what point would the gravity that taxes us toss him to the floor? He thinks of Nadine's story, of Nadine in Michael's face like a minor storm.

There is no music in Coin's family. Coin remembers a pumpkin-colored violin resting on Nadine's shoulder and his clumsy hands trying to help, and he taps his heart, thinking, Pit-a-pat. Pit-a-pat.

Michael says, "Here's what I am told, Coin. It's her body. That's what I hear. I hear that day in and day out. Nadine says, 'Whose body?' I say, 'Yours.' She says, 'I rest my case.' "

Coin says, "Meaning."

"Meaning," Michael says, "meaning it's her body. It's Nadine's baby. She says to me, 'What did you do that was so hard? Did you do something that cost you anything?' She says, 'You have five. Do you need six?' I'm to keep in mind this is her baby. I'm not to forget that. It's a fact."

Coin says, "So you abort it?"

"Me? You forgot, Coin. It's her body. You're not to forget that. She'll remind you."

Michael is standing, and Coin is sitting. Michael is trim. He says, "I'm not Superman, am I?"

They go run in the dark city, up Columbus, away from the park, and anger sits on Coin's heart. Michael, a yard out front, paces him. He has that war under his belt. Besides, his legs are stringy.

They're in street shoes. Coin flips off cars, and obscene words erupt from him. His anger struts like an imp. He runs a cab into oncoming traffic.

His feet are rocks.

Nadine takes bumpy train rides into New England. She goes to sales and closeouts, and hopes the poor will put their pointy elbows in her belly.

Michael finds her day after day on top of the refrigerator,

crouched down up there, her head two inches from the ceiling, her knees up around her ears. He wants to slap her. She holds Hops between her legs. She says, "Call me Hops, Michael." She jumps. She flings herself down, coughing, singing, "Croak, croak." He wants to kick her silly. She just comes off the refrigerator and onto the floor into a hapless spill.

"What's a word for you?" Ruth, ex-wife to Coin and mother of Nadine, says.

Coin's come with his one question. What's up with their daughter?

At the door Ruth said, "Your baby's having a baby. Rejoice."

This woman is two years older than Coin, and she sits across from him now in Levi's and cowboy boots, her hair blunt and pugnacious, saying, "Earnest," and nailing the heel of one boot to the toe of the other one.

Earnest? Coin thinks.

"To a fault," Ruth says. "Earnest to a fault." She's taking her boots off.

Her boy comes in and whispers to her. She says back to the boy, "Ask him."

The boy is seven. His name is Samuel. He belongs to Ruth and the man she is living with. Samuel says to Coin, "Do you know what time it is in L.A.?"

Coin raises his helpless hands.

"Four," Samuel says.

"A.M. or P.M.?" Coin says.

Samuel pulls Ruth to him and whispers to her. She whispers back. The boy comes up to Coin and says, "It's apples and oranges, Coin."

Coin says, "It's apples and oranges," and gets up to leave.

Ruth sets her boots down and walks him out.

He says, "The two of us, me and Nadine—we don't talk. You do, don't you? You and Nadine? Is it Michael—is there a problem with Michael?"

Ruth, angled into the doorframe, says, "Your daughter is acting like this is not the twentieth century. She's talking like she is someone's grandmother. You're her father, Coin, and she wants you to tell her what to do. And you can't. She's your baby, has always been your baby. Baby your baby, Coin."

Samuel, thigh deep in Ruth's boots and red-faced, is coming down the hall in chunky jerks. He is all joggle-eyed and is saying, "You're a good man, Coin."

Three A.M., and Coin gets a call from Nadine. She is in Massachusetts and has been to The Church of the Living God, where she did sob sob sob for a reverend. She asked him questions point-blank and put him in tears.

"The issue is not this, and the issue is not that," she says. She tells Coin the issue isn't the world, and it isn't what she wants. The issue is we are all part of God.

Coin sees her in the Sculpture Garden, circling Picasso's *She-Goat,* taking her poky steps. She is in her plum-colored coat, and sunlight is on her. She has a part in her hair he has never seen before. Her hands are deep in her pockets, and the red enamel heart marks her heart.

At what point will her mass double and send her, shoe over shoe, onto her head?

He says, "The issue is, exactly where are you?"

"No, Coin," she says. "The issue is not where am I. The issue is where am I going."

Nadine tells him she will call wherever it is.

What is the word for Nadine up there on the refrigerator, Hops between her legs, the two of them hunkered into some kind of last rite for the dead? What can Coin do for Nadine sitting there, what can he do for his daughter, who is mad enough to spit? **Q**

Power

—ZZZZZzzzzzzzzzz—

Richie, what's the matter down there, Richie? All the lights are out up here, Richie, everything, it's blown, Richie! My hair dryer doesn't work, Richie, something's off down in the socket up here! My dishwasher has a short, Richie, it's something, Richie, the same socket. I must've loaded it all up too much all up on one socket, Richie. My TV show's on tonight, you got to fix it, Richie, nothing works up here if you can't plug it in. What are you doing down there, Richie? Richie!!! I load up too much on one socket and all of a sudden my life, Richie! Better come up here, Richie! Richie??? Something's wrong, Richie, something's off, I can tell, something awful—I need you now, Richie, I do, Richie! Make things come on up here, Richie!

—ZZZZZzzzzzzzzzz—ZZZZZzzzzzzzzzz—

Richie????

What's the matter, Richie? Maybe you better come up, Richie.

Maybe we better call the power, Richie.

Can you hear me, Richie?

You give me the twitches, Richie. You do things, Richie, not just things with the fuse boxes, Richie. I don't know, Richie, so I overload for you, Richie, is that so bad?

Richie???

Oh, I got too many plugs and not enough sockets up here, Richie. But I can learn, Richie. Why not load them up, Richie? What's wrong with loading them up, Richie? It means Richie when they blow, Richie.

—ZZZZZzzzzzzzzzzzZZZZZ—

There it goes, there it blows, Richie! I told you, Richie—I can make it blow for you, Richie. Me loading, and you unload-

ing, Richie! Oh, there's always Richie. Oh, Richie, you're so—
oh, I don't know, Richie.

—ZZZZZZzzzzzzzzzzZZZZZZzzzzzzZZZZZZzzzzzz—

Say something, Richie!

Richie???

It's gone bad, hasn't it, Richie?

It's gone bad. I loaded it up too much this time, didn't I,
Richie?

I didn't know, Richie.

Richie?!???!?

Oh, Richie, Richie, show me some power, honey, show me
the light! **Q**

Pooey

"He looks so big!" Ruth said.

"Thank you," Naomi said. "We brought." She handed over a bagful of bagels.

Marx picked up Lynn's bear and bit the bear in the neck. Lynn took her finger from her mouth and made a grunting sound and pointed to the bear.

"We were worried," Tom said.

"We didn't want to wake Marx," Naomi said.

"We never wake Marx when he's asleep," Harry said. "We just wait. There's usually no hurry."

"You're here now," Ruth said.

"Yes. You're here," Tom said.

"You better let Marx keep that," Harry said.

"It's Lynn's bear," Tom said.

"We don't want Marx to get a thing about things," Naomi said.

"Let's just let Marx work through this," Harry said.

"Do you have a vacuum?" Naomi said.

"Sure," Tom said.

"Could Marx play with your vacuum?" Harry said.

"Sure," Tom said.

"Marx loves to vacuum," Harry said. "It's something we hope to cultivate in Marx."

"Vacuuming?" Ruth said.

"No—no, Ruthie," Harry said. "The work ethic—you know—the dignity of common labor."

"When did you buy these bagels?" Tom said.

"Day before yesterday," Naomi said. "They feel good on his teeth."

"*Marx*?" Tom said.

"It's his rage," Harry said.

"His what?" Tom said.

"He should be with his own parents now," Harry said. "With his own people. But we murdered them."

"We murdered *who*?" Tom said.

"We're all killers," Harry said. "We let it happen—the rape of his homeland—'*We* the *people*.'"

"I think he's dirty, Harry," Tom said.

"That's *uncool*, Marx," Harry said.

"I think we should take Marx's diaper off," Naomi said to Harry.

"We do it all the time," Harry said. "Marx hardly ever makes."

"Pooey?" Tom said.

"Have you tried these yet?" Ruth said. "They spent like a billion dollars on these."

"They look the same," Naomi said.

"They're not," Ruth said. "They're thinner and they're lighter."

"Marx doesn't need brand-name," Harry said. "Marx isn't going to get all involved with that."

"We buy generic," Naomi said.

"I guess it's okay," Tom said.

"It's cool," Harry said.

"*Marx*!" Ruth said.

"I was afraid this might happen," Harry said. "Marx is making a statement."

"Shit!" Tom said. **Q**

Altered Toys

The main thing she taught him was that blood was not a sign of pain. Watch, she had said, tearing a piece of skin away from the edge of her fingernail, squeezing blood across her tongue and from there onto her teeth. She rolled her eyes, staring at him with a pink grin, and then wiped the blood away with the back of her hand. See, she said, it had absolutely nothing to do with pain.

How late are you, exactly? he asked her. I've been stupid, she said. He pushed his fingers through her short, dark hair. But she did not look at him. I've never been particularly fertile, she told him. But this was more or less a lie.

The third time they went out, and after a big dinner, they sat on the porch of his house, sipping whiskey and watching a fight unfold in the parking lot across the street. Has it been a long time since you kissed someone? she said. He nodded, listening to a large gray car gun its engine. I am going to kiss you now, she said. You will put your hand here. He felt her pulse through his thumb. She placed her fingers on his eyes, closing them gently. There you are, she said, there, I knew I wouldn't have to do everything.

Her house was filled with carnival toys. A shotgun rested on a pedestal in one corner, rendered inoperable by the hundreds of blinking doll eyes that had been glued over every surface. A tapestry woven from her hair hung near a window, speckled with tiny pale Santa Claus faces. There were oil paintings centered around a single toy from a gumball machine, self-portraits made from partially melted toy soldiers.

Altered toys everywhere.

Whenever he could, he touched the tapestry.

Once she peered over his shoulder as he wrote. Suddenly, she pulled him backward out of his chair by his collar. He stared at her, not moving, but even so her fists caught him by surprise. She took him down and then kneeled on his chest, hissing. This is not a story, you bastard, she said.

One Halloween they were at a friend's buying a bag. They sat on a couch, smoking it and talking. Some other friends came by with the news of an accident they had seen on the highway. Bleeding clowns had been pulled from one of the cars, and two tiny children stood crying by the road with store-bought costumes on, the masks pushed up on top of their heads.

They often slept on the floor of her carpeted sun porch. One night she came in after he was already asleep, knelt down, and touched his face. I've been with another guy, she told him, peeling off her shirt, and thought you should know. Thanks, he said, and went back to sleep.

They saw one another only one more time. They exchanged hellos. As she walked away, he saw her version of the unborn child tugging at its mother's hand. His own version of the child wriggled busily in his arms. **Q**

Horn of Plenty

Toby is digging deep in the scoop, up past his elbow in this shit. I see him pull his arm out, holding a stuffed Chihuahua with an arrow stuck through its bony head. Screws jut out of its paws where it was probably once attached to something.

"Think she'll like it?" Toby says.

"Fucking A," I say, emptying a can into the back of the vehicle.

Toby runs the dog around to the front cab and drops it off. He comes back, stamping his feet and slapping his hands on his coveralls.

It is a cold one today. Fucking freezing.

"Ever find anything stranger than that?" Toby says, throwing a bundle of newspapers into the scoop.

"Sure," I say. "My wife. Found her passed out in a dumpster New Year's Day 1962. Week later we were married."

"That's a beautiful story," Toby says.

He pulls down the lever. The jaws of the truck close, crushing the crap flat.

Toby is fooling with a toaster he pulled from a can. He moves the handle up and down. He turns the toaster over and inspects the cord. It rains black crumbs and frozen roaches.

Toby has this thing of keeping all the toasters we find on the route. All of them dead, toasted out, seen their last slice of Wonder Bread. Toby thinks he can save them. He throws this junk up in the cab.

"Where you finding the room in your place for this stuff?" I say.

"I make room," Toby says. "When the baby comes is when we won't have room."

Toby heaves two black bags into the scoop. They split

open. I pick a broken cap gun from the spilled shit and click the trigger at him.

"Bang bang," I say.

Toby grabs his chest and spins backward, knocking over some empty cans.

I shove the gun in my pocket.

"Kids will like this," I say.

Toby looks away.

The horn blows. We jump on the back of the truck and hold on to the rail as it swings around the corner.

"Guess you and Wanda are still trying!" I yell over the grinding gears.

Toby nods.

"Maybe you're shooting blanks," I say, holding up a moldy head of broccoli from the scoop. "Not getting enough greens."

I see the scoop like one of those cornucopias. A horn of plenty. The kind you see in pictures around Thanksgiving with all the shit pouring out of its mouth. That is how I see the scoop, spitting out stuff for Toby and me every morning. There is always something somebody is throwing out.

My wife and I, all our dishes and forks and knives, all our books, all our wall pictures are from the scoop. I haven't had to subscribe to a magazine in years. And each night the kids search my coat for toys. Oh, we get piles of toys, Toby and me.

We look for anything that glitters. Once Toby pulled a diamond ring from coffee grinds. Turned out to be glass, but Wanda tells everyone it is the real thing. Like those earrings Toby picked from the scoop. Didn't know it but they were fishing lures without the hooks. Shit, Wanda still wears them. When someone tells her what they are, she just says big deal.

Toby has his back to me, wiping off something pink on his sleeve. I hear it rattle when he puts it in his coveralls. Hell, he catches me looking and shrugs.

"Just in case," he says.

I turn a can over into the scoop. There is a bowling ball sitting in the trash like a head. It isn't the black kind but the kind with the orangy swirls of color. I pick it up and turn it over in my hands.

"Shit," I say. "Has a crack."

I fit two fingers in the holes.

"Cough," I say.

Toby smiles. I run a hand over the ball, making crazy gestures with my eyes.

"I see the future," I say. "I see Wanda, big as a fucking balloon. I see twins."

Toby and I are almost done with the morning's loop. We found some pretty good shit today. Toby has his stuffed dog and toaster and I got a Laurel and Hardy lamp. The only thing left is to see who's going to get the blue baby we found lying in a bed of rinds. **Q**

Minoan King

Children, Mom says, children, let me teach you.

Mom takes a tablecloth and whistles for our dog. Mom gets down to her knees and reaches around under the furniture and gets our dog out by its paws. Mom bites down on one end of the tablecloth and says, Watch now, when our dog grabs on and slants back and gives a good tug. Mom holds her ground. Her gums start to bleed and tears come out of her eyes. Our dog backs away with Mom, drags her down under the furniture.

I don't think we know what the lesson is, Sister and me.

I wonder if that is him, if that is really Daddy in the black Chevy that goes slow past our house on Sunday afternoons. Mom says it most certainly is. The windows are shaded and whoever is driving never stops to show their face. One Sunday Sister walked out to the car holding Moonie, her headless doll, but the car sped off.

It is another cold Sunday afternoon.

The snowman in our front yard Sister and me made is already turning black with soot from passing cars. Sister and I kick in the stomach of the snowman. The head rolls off and splits into big snow chunks. We throw the chunks at our dog, who snaps them into white powder.

Mom comes out bundled up and sits on the porch and waits for the black Chevy.

I hope Daddy doesn't drive by today. Mom seems restless. I picture her throwing her big body on the hood of the Chevy, digging her nails into it and not letting go until Daddy stops and shows himself and pays our bills.

Here comes the Chevy. Mom lifts a hand and waves.

She says, Wave to your father, children.

I wave and lift Sister's wrist and flap her small mittened hand in the air.

The Chevy rolls on until next week.

It is early morning and someone is rapping hard on our front door. From my room I hear the dog in a frenzy on the kitchen floor and Mom's bare feet running across the linoleum. Then I hear a man's voice explaining our problem, wanting money from us.

Take this matter up with my husband, Mom yells and slams the door.

Bastards, Mom says. Scum.

It is already late in the day this Sunday and no black Chevy. We are out of hot chocolate, so Mom gives us coffee. Sister and I sip our coffee and Mom sits at the kitchen table with her crosswords.

We hear a snap and the oil burner rumbles down to a stop. Mom doesn't look up from her puzzle.

Twelve down, she says, a Picasso daughter.

Then the light over the kitchen table flickers and goes out.

Twenty-five across, Mom says, female goat.

So we sit listening to the cars, waiting for one to slow down and maybe pull up our drive and pay the bills because Mom won't pay them. She says that is our father's job. But our father is not here. He is gone. Left laughing his way out the screen door while Sister and I were dragging the Christmas tree box out from under the stairs and our mother sat at the kitchen table saying, fourteen across—Minoan king. **Q**

They Were Naked Again

In an instant she may not see it as it happens, how light crowds in and around her red hair, and all around her head, before vanishing into some other light, which is likely having nothing more to do with her hair?—but this is wrong, because there is no inkling of science.

So—I'll get her into his bed, looking at his carpet, which is on his floor, rolled up. Together, they look at it, not for any reason they guess might augment them.

He is prepared to get rid of the carpet. It has been causing him to feel bereft of something he probably never had—something which I could give him.

I could.

She says, "Please don't get rid of it. It comforts me."

I would never say that to him. I would never say that to him in this situation, which is a situation which is a spectacular opportunity for them both, and it is my time they are taking.

You know what happens when they both are thinking so much about the carpet at the same time?

His experience appears to be one of elation, such as finishing. Then she says something obscene, which happens to be clairvoyant. Then I say, "I gave my own carpet away like that, *bitch!*"

But they cannot hear me.

I'll threaten suicide!

You—you think about a carpet.

Me. **Q**

Meat

The prince's house makes me feel respect for his house. The house causes me to stand and look at his house as if his house deserves all of my attention. I will need to be butted out of this drifting off into full respect for his house by something necessary or urgent, and nobody will get me to speak about my mother's new boyfriend instead of the prince who lives in this house.

The first time I met the prince, he was talking to his hired man inside of my neighbor's garage, and he told me to come by sometime and we could have an Ovaltine at his house.

I just don't want to say why we were all in the garage. It is not even as germane as the rumpled prince on the edge of his property today, talking with the three hired men. His hair, his shirt, his trousers were rumpled.

There was a rather smooth aspect to the shirt of one of the hired men, how it stretched itself smoothly down, then down in under and behind his belt, which reminds me of the food galore at my mother's boyfriend's party, which an overweight woman dressed in white with bleached yellow hair prepared and served to us—meat.

I loved Gwen—the woman sitting next to me at the party. She bakes her bread in a machine. It doesn't swirl, but since it is better to be impetuous, she puts into it anyway cinnamon and raisins into the white dough!

I am tempted to not say anything more which could imply anything, because this is not literature. This is espionage.

N.B. If you like, change all the words. **Q**

Nude

The parrot's owner gives me information about the parrot that the parrot is molting, or something that is awful—that it hates women. The parrot's owner is also a treasure-house of information about libidinous debauches.

The parrot's owner should be a handsome man. He has wrapped himself in a white bath towel. His hair is wet.

His little girl is sort of chirping *She hates me! I just hate her!* about their parrot, as a little girl will. She sort of bounces brightly in her swimsuit with its dots of purplish blue and reddish purple, and purplish pink.

I am wearing my brand-new nude—what the shop owner called the nude. The slip has a crease running down its center, not between my legs, from its having been all folded up inside of a drawer in the shop before I took it to try on.

I bought a robe, too, from that shop, which I could have had in any one of three different colors—which I will not name—the colors. But I could have.

However, when the shop owner spoke to me of under-clothes the color of pink ice, I sort of lost hope that I would ever get them, but I have imagined nothing strong or deep or vivid or very dark or bluish in all the pricks I will have.

How could I?

How could I?

How could I? **Q**

Teeth

He is filled with Valium, codeine, and Carbocaine, and he can hear himself breathing in the corner near the ceiling. He is expanding, filling the house so that the walls will crack open and he will spill onto the street.

"They said to take out the gauze and drink a milk shake even if it bleeds." Arlene in her high-top tennis shoes says from the hallway. Arlene brings the McDonald's bag to him and she holds out her arm.

He gets up from the bed and goes to the bathroom to take out the gauze, and he sees that his face is swollen and covered with hair. He started turning into an animal on the way home from the oral surgeon's when Arlene stopped for soft foods and a group of high-school girls laughed at him, his mouth stuffed open with gauze.

He goes to the kitchen, where Arlene is sitting at the table doing the crossword, her thin forearms resting on the newspaper. He has to pour the milk shake into his mouth and let some dribble onto a towel, and he tastes the rusty taste of his own blood.

The dental hygienist phones and Arlene answers. Arlene balances on one heel, and she slides a pencil back and forth on top of her ear. Then she sits back down.

"She wanted to know if you were bleeding a lot. What is the name for thatching grass and a sodium symbol?" Arlene says.

He goes back into the bathroom and puts more gauze in the bleeding sockets where his teeth used to be. The teeth that are left are long and pointed, and there is a filmy membrane over his eyes. He goes to the bedroom and lies on the bed, his thick brown nails clutching at the sheet.

"Aren't you going to take off your jacket?" Arlene says from the hallway. "You should at least take your jacket off."

He falls asleep. When he wakes, it is dark. He can taste more blood and he can see a black place on the pillow where he has been bleeding in his sleep. He turns on the lamp and he sees that there is blood down the front of the hair on his chest. He searches for the gauze in his mouth and he realizes that he has swallowed it in his sleep, nearly choked to death on it. Arlene has left him to die.

Bitch.
Cunt.
Blond bitch-cunt with her scraggly pink pubic hair.
He goes to the kitchen and he finds the bag with the codeine. Arlene comes into the kitchen, her face marked from the couch and her hair flat on one side. She looks at his face and gasps. He drops the bag, goes to Arlene, and pulls her next to him. Smashing Arlene's lung against his, he can feel the blood straining to move inside Arlene's veins.

Arlene flutters.
Then she stops fluttering for good. **Q**

Nose

My kid Wesley had been acting out since the divorce—doing things like holding something out for me and dropping it just before I get there. When I had someone over, or talked on the phone, Wes made fart noises and laughed the kind of laugh that sounds like it's coming from a pull-string doll. The psychiatrist said going on a vacation would help. Wes and I had never been on a vacation—not the kind where you pick a place to go and make reservations. The people where I worked said we should go try it around San Diego. I called a few travel agencies but they didn't want to bother with small stuff, so I called 411 and asked for anything that started with San Diego. So that's how we got to that particular motel.

Wes slept all the way there and woke up with his asthma. I gave him his medicine, then went to a store for sandwich stuff. It wasn't too bad of a place—the motel. There were little window boxes with flowers and you could sit outside and bar-beque or read a book.

In the morning Wes and I walked along the wharf and went out to where people were standing around a sign that said Ship's Bell—$1.50. So we got in line with the others, and after a while the man there took our money and told everyone to get in. Then he closed the thing up and stood out there looking at us while the bell lifted off the pier and started going down and I was holding on and thinking about Wes and how he would have something to tell his friends when we got back. It was real stuffy inside the bell and I could smell the hairspray of somebody right away.

"Where are we going?" Wes said.

"To the bottom of the ocean," I said.

We settled down with a terrible noise on the ocean floor. For a while I couldn't see anything. Then someone said they saw a rock. We all moved to the side where you could see the rock. My head started to hurt and I was already feeling sick. I wanted to open a window.

"Look at the seaweed," I said to Wes, pointing to something. But Wes was too short and I had to lift him.

"Is this all there is down here?" he said.

The guy who was in charge of the bell in there with us gave us a little smile.

"How long do we have to be in this thing?" Wes said.

There were some biker guys in there and they were pretending to kick each other with their army boots. They looked pretty smashed to me. You could smell their B.O.

"Let's see if we can see anything on the other side," I said, guiding Wes.

"Nothing good ever happens to us," Wes said.

"You'd think there would be more down here to see," some bitch said.

"We're too close to shore," her boyfriend said.

"He got a fucking tape measure or something?" one of the bikers says.

"Just another tourist trap," the bitch says.

"We're such suckers," her boyfriend says.

"Who's a sucker?" one of the bikers says.

He looked pretty crazy to me.

"Shake it off," one of the other ones says.

"Sucker fucker," Wes says, and starts poking at my leg and making static sounds.

"Tell your kid to shut up," one of the bikers says.

"Let's count the fish," I said to Wes.

The air was getting worse. But I kept telling myself they'd pull us up soon.

"Sucker fucker," Wes says again.

The official guy, he gets out his nail clippers and starts to clip his nails.

"I wonder if they have whales down here?" the bitch says.

"Too close to the shore," the boyfriend says.

No one said anything for a while. Then the bitch says, "Oh, look, everyone, I think I see something!" Everyone goes to her side again and looks out the fucking window.

"Scrap metal from one of the houseboats," her boyfriend says.

"Well, it could have been a whale," the bitch says.

The official guy keeps clipping his nails. Guys like this always look stupid to me, like they don't have anything on their minds except nookie.

"How long have you been doing this?" I said.

"Forget it," the guy says.

"I hate this," Wes says.

I look down and see his lips are getting swollen like the way they do before he gets his asthma.

"This is certainly long enough for anyone in his right mind to be on the ocean floor," the bitch says.

"Maybe they've forgotten about us," the boyfriend says.

"Shush," the woman slaps his arm. "There's a child here, you know," she says.

"They forgot about us?" Wes says.

"He wants to make sure we see everything," I said.

"The asshole's probably off somewhere getting some ginch," one of the bikers says.

Wes gets down on the floor and starts bumping his head against the side. "We're going to die," he says.

"Even if the man did go off somewhere," the bitch says, "new people will come and want to ride. They'll go into one of the shops—there must be a manager of all the shops on the pier."

"Will you shut the fuck up!" one of the bikers says.

The boyfriend just looks at the bikers. Wes is kicking his legs at people.

"This kid want me to hand him his head?" the biker says.

"He has asthma," I said. "I forgot his medicine."

The bitch kneels down. "Never you mind," she says to

Wes. "We'll be up on top in a minute and you will feel ever so much better."

"Sucker fucker!" Wes yells.

"He fucking talking to me?" the biker says.

I sit down on the floor next to Wes. His breath smells pretty lousy, the way it does before he stops breathing.

"Maybe we could signal to the guy we're ready," I said.

"I bet I know someone who needs a nap," the bitch says.

"Get me some Coke to drink!" Wes screams.

"Anybody got any playing cards?" the boyfriend says.

One of the bikers punches him right in the face. Served the fucker right. I told him so when we got back up on the pier and were getting out. But I pictured the bitch taking the motherfuck back to their room and them having a few gins together. Maybe they would watch a little TV, and she would go to the store and buy a couple of rib-eyes to barbeque on the patio. Later on, she'd probably give him some head to make up for the nose. **Q**

Pilgrim

Yow had eaten a sugar cube of acid an hour before. He had timed the acid to start hitting him right as they would be making their getaway. Only there had been several unforeseen complications. Everything now seemed hysterically funny. They seemed to be actors in a movie. The lighting in the store was phenomenally bright, and Yow was a little worried about the possibility of going blind. There wasn't a spot in the entire store that wasn't shiny, and light was reflecting off of every surface.

"Please," an old woman begged.

"Shut up or die," Vic said.

It was 9:30 in the morning. A Tuesday; the beginning of the end of a long summer; Northeast Dallas. From the instant the five of them walked in with their shotguns and revolvers, it had been a disaster. An old woman had started screaming when Moore ran down the aisle with his shotgun; and one of the locals they'd hired had slipped on the freshly polished floor, and the manager had used the distraction to run right out the front door. Yow had emptied his .38 in a wild arc of fire at the front windows, hitting the manager in the leg and spraying him with glass; but the son of a bitch managed to get out to his car and speed away before they could kill him. Yow thought to run straight out the front door, but Moore and Vic were in the back—Yow could hear yelling—and it didn't sound like they were coming out. Then the acid went off in a fast phosphorescent flash and suddenly everything became outrageously funny. He reloaded his gun as he gingerly strolled to the back, thinking himself in the Old West, about to blow some faggot marshal's dick off. And that fucking manager. That walleyed coot was about as shit-scared as anyone he'd ever seen. And all that glass flying! Yow felt himself riding a wave of ultimate cool.

Vic pointed the shotgun at the butcher's freshly washed apron. Vic hated the man's eyes. He wondered if he could get a blast off into those eyes without causing pandemonium.

The two incompetent hicks they'd hired were freaking out. They'd been too scared to run, and now they were too scared to hang tough. They were as fidgety and edgy as girls. Moore went over and said something to them and they both straightened up a bit, but then almost immediately started freaking out again. Moore turned and glared at them but seemed to be enjoying himself, as if this was the exact situation he'd always wanted to be in.

They were in the extreme rear of the store. Everybody standing near the frozen sausage and canned hams. They had eleven hostages in all and there were by now at least that many police cars outside.

Moore ambled over to Vic, lazily carrying the shotgun, a Sears .410. "They used to have this place outside of Houston," he started saying, like they were in a bar somewhere and had all the time in the world. "Texas Rangers would bring their prisoners there. Place called the Windmill."

Vic looked quickly around, eyeing the assistant manager, a few ancient retirees, a woman in her thirties, a girl in a stylish haircut.

"They'd tie a guy up there," Moore went on, intent with the story, "and when cops got off duty, they'd swing by and beat the shit out of the guy for a while. The guy couldn't do anything, he was all tied up. I celled with this guy in Florida— old guy—looked old anyway—he'd been there. Face was just scar tissue. They'd worked on him for three days." Vic looked at Moore. Vic's face nervous and sweaty. Moore laughed. Drew a hand through his light, close-cropped hair, turning to the woman with the scarf, "That your daughter?"

The woman nodded in terror. Moore called Yow over.

"Get some baby oil or Vaseline. Something like that." A ripple of horror ran across the faces. "Why aren't any of you suntanned?" Moore asked them. "It's the middle of fucking August and you're white as ghosts."

Moore handed his shotgun over to Vic, who now held both weapons trained on the butcher and the assistant manager. Moore said, "Vic, tell me something. Have you ever in your life been really laid? I mean laid straight out, all the way to the end?"

Vic grinned maniacally. "No, man, just hogs, my whole fucking life."

Yow ran up with a bottle of baby oil. "You," Moore said to the woman's skinny ten- or eleven-year-old daughter with the haircut. "Pants *down.*"

"Drop 'em!" Yow yelled out, laughing.

The girl shook off a recalcitrant blond curl that had fallen down on her forehead, then slipped down her jeans, and, without being asked, got out of her underpants. The kid acted stoned, sky-high, beyond fear.

Moore rubbed some oil up her ass, squeezing his middle finger in to the knuckle. Outside someone was speaking into a megaphone, saying he was going to do this, do that, we've got you now, look out. Then Moore took a shotgun shell and forced that into the kid's ass, laughing, his body shaking with mirth, happy in its element. He pulled out a Walther 9mm automatic—a small, funny-looking weapon with a chipped wooden handle—and inserted the tip of it into the girl's anus. The girl stood ludicrously bent over, hands on knees, eyes glazed, some insane parody of a Coppertone ad.

"Now," Moore said, "how do we get out of here?"

They were running, they were running, they were running, and when they came to the quiet suburban street, shotguns bobbing, they saw her at the same instant she saw them. She stood at the end of a driveway. They'd been running for two miles with Moore praying his knee wouldn't give out, and when they hit the parkway, they dug their feet into the grass to try and slow themselves down—the woman staring wide-eyed. She gave them one of those looks a person only gives out once in a lifetime, a look with everything behind it, and she ran straight toward the front door, only seventy-five feet away, but Moore fired, and then Vic fired, and then Moore fired again—a boom boom boom of shotgun blasts catching her between the shoulders, back of the head, and in the ass as she was propelled forward, and they picked up speed again as she finally skidded facedown on the driveway. Vic and Moore laughed, choking, trying to breathe, holding their sides with their free hands, then reloading, dropping shells on the lawns, coughing, laughing, staggering, running along. Then cutting across a corner lawn, poodle yapping in a window, another boom boom boom as they triple-blasted it to smithereens, and then went slamming up the block, through a hedgerow, and out to the highway.

They walked up Collins to 65th Street and the Brazil Hotel, where they played a few high-energy games of shuffleboard by the filthy pool. Yow shrieked with delight every time he sent one of Moore's ten-point ringers into the grass with a whoooooosh. Vic tossed around a few packets of Sweet'n Low filled with high-grade and they all dipped in their plastic McDonald's straws and blew their pain away. When all the packets were finished, Moore lay back on a rusty lounge chair and said, "Christ, will you look at that moon!"

Inside room 211, with the radio turned to country and western and the dresser barricaded against the door, Yow pinned the nigger against the bedroom wall, his hand pressed in on her throat.

Yow said, "I know what you are, and I know the kinds of sewers you've rimmed and sucked in, and I also know that this is going to be about the best tail you ever threw, because the last bitch that turned us wrong we blew into about seven hundred pieces."

The nigger was cool. She'd dealt with this kind before. She slowly let out her wet, shiny, pointed, heavenly, cocksucker's tongue and began hummingbirding it until it was nothing but a dreamy blur. "Honey," she said, "you gonna feel so good, I'm gonna take you to a place that so high."

She undid Yow's pants.

Moore and the kid laughed in the corner. **Q**

The Kid with His Mind in the Sewer

I

Five mornings of every week I listened to him court his girl friend with the nose and the braces on her teeth. They were all giggles and jabs. She was whispery quiet. He was a stubby little loudmouth playing to the whole bus for her. His daily refrain was, "I guess I was born with my mind in the sewer." He was always trying to sniff out who had just farted. She giggled and snuggled against him into spring. She went to a Catholic school downtown. He went somewhere else. As the weather got warm, I began to walk and forgot about the kid with his mind in the sewer and the retarded guy with his paper-bag briefcase trying to sell me a water filtration system. I mean, the kid might have become a little likeable if he had bought the filtration system and worn it like a hat.

II

By fall it was over. She had lost weight, grown two inches, had her braces taken off, and was now almost pretty. She wanted nothing to do with him. She was busy studying when he hopped on the bus with his swagger and smirk. His questions went unanswered. His games had no partner. I heard her tell him to "grow up." I heard her tell him about this "neat guy" she had met. The kid fought back. He tried to act intelligent. He became well versed in public television. His class was reading *The Merchant of Venice*. (That's by Shakespeare.) But she didn't care about a pound of flesh. She was "going out" now. Was he "going out" with anyone? She looked at him only when she asked him something that made him shrink. She had put a blond rinse in her hair and was getting shapelier by the day. I couldn't help but feel sorry for the little jerk. He was too young to have lost already the thing he could never have. You should be at least twenty before that happens to you.

III

His Safeway name tag identified him as KURT. In two years he had almost grown a mustache. Otherwise, he was the same dwarfish, insolent kid with kinky hair and the bad skin. Bagging my groceries, he seemed mad at the inequity of his having managed to get a job. Behind me, three rough-looking lesbians were reading aloud selected headlines from the tabloids. They seemed to take the most pleasure in mocking the stories of women in distress. WOMAN GIVES BIRTH TO ALIEN LOVE CHILD. SWAMI SACRIFICES LOVE SLAVES TO REACH NIRVANA. I took my bag from Kurt and walked out the door past a skinny black woman on the pay phone. "Shit," she was saying, "I don't know nobody else who going to loan me the money."

IV   *Last Thing About the Kid with his Mind in the Sewer*

I was surprised when I heard voices outside. It was just the beginning of dawn. I felt a moment of fear. I didn't want to see something horrible. I peered out along the window frame. It had stormed all night and left pools of standing water in the street. The kid with his mind in the sewer was passing under the streetlight. I could hear him in an argument with somebody who was not there. **Q**

On the Job

I

"Quick question?" she says, standing in my doorway, her mechanical pencil poised firmly against a yellow tablet. It isn't ten yet. She's already been by once. There's an electronic mail message from her queued up on my terminal. I've been ignoring it while I watch the bridge open for a tugboat. She wants to know whether the department standard is to put a comma before *too* when it comes at the end of a sentence. I tell her it doesn't matter. Finally I let her read me the sentence: *The field definitions have been revised too.* "No comma," I say. She writes it down and underlines it twice. Then she gives me this smirky, conspiratorial glance. "Between you and me," she says, "I wouldn't have put it in either."

I I

She has two rabbits she walks around on a leash. Bernie and Morris. Last week she told me she "used to be a feminist." She's afraid the corporation might find out. Before that she was a party girl living in Hawaii with her hair down to her you-know-what. Along the way she has done "serious research" on the semicolon. One day she's going to bring in her notes and show me where the experts go both ways.

I I I

We ride the elevator down to the mezzanine. She's seen something in one of the shops she wants to buy. It's a wind-up rabbit. She collects rabbit items. It's her theme. Put a rabbit on something or put something in the shape of a rabbit and she buys it. "Quality makes no difference," she says.

"I'm obsessed." In a month I have to recommend whether she be kept. Everyone is always kept. All day I'm thinking about ways to tell her tactfully that all she has to do to get on permanent here is to stop being nuts.

IV

She comes into the conference room loaded down with manuals. The manuals are bulky to begin with and they're stretched out of their binders because she's got every fifth page paper-clipped. She has a list of twelve questions. A list of five concerns. Seven inconsistencies. She sits down across from me. "I'm not a tinkerer," she says.

V

She wants me to explain the processing differences between the four kinds of fees on the Commercial Lending System. "You don't need to know that," I say. She reads them off to me: accruing, fixed, prepaid amortizing, prepaid direct-to-income. "I want to get where I'm just like you," she says. "I want to know everything just like that." She snaps her fingers. Then makes a fist. She seems to be threatening me with it. Last week she got her hair cut short. Now it fits around her thin face like a helmet and makes her look sinister. "Have you ever been married?" she asks me. When I say I haven't, she leans forward with that secret-agent squint of hers and tells me she was married once. He was a hunk. But she got that out of her system. Q

Karl and Ilse

A pair of canvas chairs before the ocean as on some dim stage before a vacancy of seats, not drama.

She had complained of biting flies and gone inside.

He had walked along the beach to the reeds and slow waters, lowland, where he had seen the duck, its strange-seeming behavior. First a turning of its head to one side, then a twisting up, and finally an opening of the beak and stretching as if not to yawn but to swallow painfully or to gasp. It did not swim. Floated with leaves and wash in eddies among the broken reeds in the marsh. It lifted one wing, jerked it up as if bitten, thrashed, stopped and held the wing extended, then lowered it a little, slowly, and tried to strike at it with its foot. Finally the bird settled into a kind of stillness, its head sunk low and the one wing still not fully placed, the feathers ruffled and the wing askew.

After a while he walked back along the beach to the chairs. His towel lay here, dropped across a chairback. He touched it, but did not take it. Walked up to the cottage.

"How useless this life," Ilse said after he had come into the room. She sat at the kitchen table, her legs spread and skirt sunk between them. She held a paper fan. "That we should travel so far to be overcome by insects."

Karl stared at her, the gray light around her and the ground boards of the floor, her thin nose and quick hands.

"What is there to eat?"

"Nothing. There is nothing to eat because there are flies everywhere. There is no way to prepare food without washing and cleaning."

"I will fix something."

"No."

"It is good to eat."

"You are always the same," she said. "Do something different. Don't eat."

"I have my consistency."

"Don't."

"It is natural."

"Deny it. Feel hunger."

"Will you come back down to the beach?"

"No."

A fly darted at the broken screen. A moth flew across the room. Gnats swirled.

"We have come to a forlorn place, the end of the earth."

"Sancho Panza says that all ills are good with food."

"Had he ever lived, Sancho Panza would be dead. There are welts on the backs of my hands. I must put on more clothing to be covered and to perspire in."

"There are trains in this country. We will take a train."

"Why?"

"To leave here if you want."

"For the dining car?"

"For the train."

"We came by bus."

Blackbirds tore seeds from heads of dune grass, the stalks bending. An old moon was white in the sky. Wind carried sand across the porch and under the door. Karl turned from Ilse. He went out. The small waves that ran slowly up the beach did not wash back again but drained down, subsiding through the coarseness of gravel and sand.

When Ilse came out, she had veiled herself, a wide brimmed hat and a swath of netting wrapped around it trailing over her face and head and tucked beneath a dark blouse. On her hands, there were white cotton gloves.

"Where are the people?" she asked. "Furs around them and taking meat out of this ocean."

"They left when the flies came."

"They do not bite you?"

"They do."

"You have no blood, no flesh."

"I have had it for you."

"Ha. You say that. Always the same."

"I say it because of you."

"You hunger for me?"

"Yes."

"I do not believe you."

"It is true."

"Say it."

"I hunger."

"You know nothing about truth."

"There is truth in everything everywhere."

"Say it."

"I hunger."

A button at the neck of Ilse's blouse had come undone where the netting was thrust in. He glimpsed the skin of her through the veil.

"Why are we left alone?"

He put his hand on her arm, cotton and flesh. She turned from him.

Karl saw her by stream, slough, and reeds, and he again saw the duck turning in shallows of wash and still foam. Its head remained low and fallen, the one wing trailing.

At last the sun was low.

Ilse turned away from the beach.

"I will show you," she said.

This was as far north as they could come, this strange cold ocean. He heard the casting and wash of gravel, imagined an eddy of reeds and feather.

"I am in love with being alive."

Karl entered the water, waves and sea. Arches. Vaults. He waded at first. To the south, stars and cold air. He waded farther, then swam, losing contact with the earth at the point he had given to walking bent forward to the seas, there becoming a swimmer.

Horizon.

Seal and bear. Petrels.

Distance.

Ice.

At the lift of the sun, the duck preened again, then flew away.

Ilse left by train.

Karl waded ashore where the current had taken him, released from it cold, thick as invisible swirl in gel where it eddied past a thrust of broken rock and low headland. He lay awhile in faint wash at the edge of the reach of waves, the warmest he could find the merge of air and water until he was able to go farther in, scoop at sand, dig himself into dune grass and earth, warmest there. He saw above him a small house of cast timbers and driftwood. A blanket had been left on a rail at the crude porch. He slipped up, took it and wrapped himself in it, then lay again in the grass. He watched the house.

First the smell of it, then a little smoke at the chimney, until a woman appeared, long-haired and fair, her breasts loose in some casual wrap.

How beautiful in garments. **Q**

Dance, Mice, Dance!

He wasn't just scared of mice. He was scared of every-thing. Sometimes he was in his garden, gardening. He would have the sensation that one of the plants was going to wrap around his arm. Or that the worms might suck him under the ground; that some strange, biting, poisonous insects would sting, bite, and eat him. Rotten food was also scary. He didn't watch horror movies, but he knew how they worked.

One day, mice came to his home. He woke up and he could hear them, chewing inside his wall. He lived on the second floor and he figured they must've chewed their way up from the first. He could barely hear them in there. He had to be very still, hardly breathe.

He wanted to put his ear up to the wall, but he saw teeth, giant teeth with slobber, tearing through the wall and sucking his head in. He shuddered, laying in his bed. He was sweating. And the mice kept chewing. He could hear them. They could eat through his wall and eat the wires on his stereo. Then his records, then his clothes.

These mice, he thought.

He saw himself with a gun, a big gun—two of them—in holsters. He had spurs. Mice were on the other side of the road. "Draw," he said, and then started shooting at the mice, guns-a-blazing-style. "Dance, mice, dance!" he said, aiming at their little feet, watching them hop up and down.

I'm sick of being pushed around, he thought. I'm sick of being polite. These are mice, he thought. I'm a human, he thought, and humans rule!

He cautiously got up from his bed and tip-toed over to the wall. He leaned down. With his heart racing, he put his ear to the wall. He heard chewing.

And plates clicking together—and chairs being pushed

around. And drinks being poured. He saw a mouse in an apron.

Then there was no noise at all for a moment.

Then there was noise again.

Must've said Grace, he thought. **Q**

Three Stories

I

"I think I'm going to cut my hair short," he said, looking at himself in the mirror.

"What?" I said. "How short?"

"And I'm going to dye it blond." He turned his head to the side, pulling the hair out of his face.

I touched him on the arm and he flinched away, still looking in the mirror.

"And I'm changing my name to David," he said.

He turned to me, and I could see that his eyes were red again.

"Don't you think it's a nice name?" he said.

"Don't," I said, "please, don't."

But he was already gone, looking for the scissors.

II

He opened the door, and she said "I came to get my friend's purse. She left it here last night."

He looked at her and blinked.

"Oh—yes, she did leave it here. How's she doing this morning?" he said.

"Fine," the woman said. "Just give me the purse."

"Yes," he said.

He went inside and came back with the soft black leather. She took it from him and walked away.

"Asshole," he heard her say under her breath.

III

Last night I dreamed I was driving with Kafka in the passenger seat. I went around the bend in the road and saw a little girl in a coat in my lane and a car coming at us. I wasn't going very fast, but the road was icy. If I jammed on the brakes, I would have just slid into her and killed her. So instead I stopped the dream, and got out.

It is like avoiding responsibility, which I also do in life. **Q**

Not Home

THE POOL

It is overcast, so there aren't so many people around. Everyone here is rich and harmless, no ambition. It's just a Holiday Inn somewhere on a coast. It's before summer. It's still cool. I've been sleeping hours and hours and hours a night, Elizabeth and I, watching the news, some nights, before falling asleep. We hold hands, going down, falling under.

But in the day Elizabeth swims. I should swim, too, but I am frightened of the water. These are the ways I have lately been dreaming of death—a car wreck (which is the worst) or drowning (which I used to think was the worst, but which I no longer do).

So much metal, dead by cars.

It makes me feel hopeful, and proud, that Elizabeth is the only truly attractive—physically—person around the pool. I don't mean that is the only way to look at a person, but when I see so many people—everyone—being out of shape, and uncaring about it, it makes me feel—tired.

Elizabeth finishes her swim, climbs out of the pool, is wet and healthy.

"Bodybuilders are almost as terrible to look at as the fat people are," she says. "They're all scary."

Down at the far end there are a couple of big fellows sitting in chairs, hoping for sun, I guess—though I also guess none is coming. It's a nice, balmy, overcast, sunless day.

THE PATIO

Earlier, when I was sitting by myself, sipping coffee and reading, I saw a woman in a bathing suit throwing up in the bushes: hacking, retching. Oh, God, she was bending over and putting her finger in her mouth, making herself do it. It was pretty early in the morning, and I don't think the woman knew I was watching her. I think she must have been on a vacation, too. She had red hair, a white body; and the swimsuit, it was black. She was just gagging and heaving. She must have eaten a lot at supper the night before, and then maybe at breakfast, too. After a while the sound of it, just going on and on, didn't sound so bad to me. It sounded a little like a lion in a little jungle.

I bet the woman thought she was hidden, but I could see her, standing out in the ferns and palms like that, barefooted, like Eve in the early, misty morning—and the people in the restaurant, behind the dark-tinted plate glass windows, they must have been able to see her, too.

THE BEACH

It hurts my knees to walk on the beach too far, but we do it anyway, while the dogs, frenzied at the eternal strip of land, race up and down the ocean's edge, chasing crabs, rolling and fighting. It's dusk, and there is no one around, not in any direction, for as far as we can see, which is a long way. Just the four of us—Elizabeth and me and the dogs, who catch the crabs sometimes, and toss them back and forth like toys.

THE JETTY

Those dreams: it is a strange and bad thing, to begin having them for the first time in your life, the kind where you really believe, if you're easily spooked—as I am, when I'm tired—that they're a premonition of the coming day.

There is never any noise, nor any blinding flash of light: just a silent emptiness, at the end of the dream, like fog, like an empty, empty movie theatre. It is so different from what I hear is everyone else's end-of-life vision (smell of bread, shining light, etc.) that it worries me that maybe mine is the right one: me sitting alone in an empty movie theatre, but with no movie to ever come, and no one to ever come in and sit down. Just sitting, and waiting.

I had to rest my knees. It's dark, and the stars are out, and now when we get back I can order drinks for us, the kinds you can drink on vacation at the beach. With no one else on the beach, all this beach, we can walk like the first ones born.

THE RESTAURANT

I have lost a lot of weight in these last months. The seafood's good, and so are the desserts, and the coffee. The buffet is styled upon the premise "All You Care To Eat," and at the dessert table I scrape off almost all—almost every bit— of some cake's icing, because the icing is the only part I care to eat. We giggle like teenagers, Elizabeth and I, back at our table: we laugh until we are crying, a little, until there are tears coming down our cheeks. I don't know. It seems something you can do on a vacation, to brand it as a vacation.

THE ROOM

We've rented bikes, and ridden slowly on winding trails beneath shady live oaks. All these old people, all these rich people—or soft young people, with children. Whereas we're still hard and violent and young, Elizabeth and I, and, certainly, so are our wild dogs. Or is that how the other people see us, too: as being as soft as they are? Are we giving off our true nature, or do they see us wrong?

My God, we're so young and hard!

The hum of the air conditioner. Deep, tumbling, mid-day naps, and the room ice-cold—while outside, the sun is shining, it is bright daytime, and no one tries the beach.

It is safe to sleep.

We are going to wake up. **Q**

The commute

Au 90

The Warning

Every morning there is a conflagration
of twenty peaks,
and the sun flies up from behind them
growing hotter and smaller,
straining to disappear
into its vehement heart.
Nearly as old

as my dead mother, I cannot keep myself
from warning her
she is about to die. All day
I consider strategies, suspecting the dead
to be set in their ways, difficult
to warn, and warned,

probably scornful. I recall
no detail of her face, only
a smudge of eye or of nostril, perhaps
the shadow of a hand. I am desperate

to be understood, but we are caught
between existences. Though she does not fail
to listen, she seems not to hear,
and speaks to me at all times

in her ordinary voice
about nothing at all. Whereas
the terrible knowledge I propose
lacerates my tongue,
her calm voice answers *nothing*
nothing nothing

The Land of Heart's Desire

Eriugena caught the sound of God
coming to him one night from a lost moon
that hid itself behind a drumlin wood
not long before the sun came back again.
This was the music light makes over Ireland,
as jackdaws toss themselves like chips of slate
over gray lake water under a smear of sky,
their cursive wingbeats writing nothing down.
Maybe he thought this was the song God made
the night the moon came out for the first time
to put light in the place of that much sky
that otherwise was dark without the moon.
All this is set forth in a book he wrote
in the ninth century for the king of France,
who never understood a thing he meant,
but sat and drank and watched the moon go down
just before cockcrow, a long way from Ireland.

The Queen of Heaven

His craving for the flesh of Mary Quinlan
had faded softly into dumb disuse.
Now and again he walked down the boreen
beside her cottage in the aspen copse,
and he could draw up from his soul the dream
of moss as bright as ginger among her thighs,
where he could leap like a great frog after a rain.
The way in was a low path under branches,
and there were nettles in the ditch beside,
but Mary Quinlan sang to the sweet winds
that nudged the curtains at the kitchen window
where he might see her shadow in the lace
or take her song and carry it on his way
up to the bridge to croon it to the river.
A gang of blackbirds bickered from the poplars.
One Friesian uttered forth a burst of spray,
blessing the buttercups. He kept on singing.
The sound rose like a noise among the nations,
a lovecry from the heart's embitterment,
the loin's remorse for sweetness kept away,
where gray walls showed the Virgin and her child
a blue fly on the lampshade by the bed.

Summer in Umbria

I used to sit down drunk on my front porch
to watch the afternoon and the mulberry

mingle together with timbrels and dances
to the wind chime's ruthless tinkle, as if the sun

could leap and kick his heels around that tree
in her small gown of green, beside the shadow

because it was not the light I wanted there,
but other light that stood among cypresses

beyond a garden with fig trees and cicadas
jangling above the voices of young girls

who stopped to take their shoes off by the gate
so they could dance home barefoot from there on.

The Ape of Emain Macha

The king at Emain Macha had an ape
which someone brought to him from Africa.
This was a Barbary ape, whose skull was found
when the great mound was opened, along with
    brooches,
trumpets, other bones of pigs and cattle—
nothing unusual, except for the ape's skull,
and a man's skull, also, severed down the middle.

I lay on top of that great dome over Ulster,
and watched two blackbirds drifting near the sun.
They made a pair of rings, one on the other.
I heard the roar of the king's boy-warriors
striving with Cuchulain on the Armagh road.
The king's ape leaped and screamed with terrible
    joy
to see the blood of children spilt for fun.

This Woman

These extra pounds aren't me,
this tired dress,
these vinyl shoes.
I'm not this woman
walking into this house.

> I'm the undeveloped film
> found in the basement.
> I'm the secret pocket in jeans.

No one knows.
My children fight over grapes.
My husband sets his watch.

> I change colors.
> Tonight I'm turquoise
> just before it deepens.

The Church of San Solitudo

I am an abbot.
My cassock is ceramic, and my finger bears a
    golden molar.
Visitors kiss it.
Visitors are unwelcome in my walls.
When my limestone sighs for me, my demons wake
    and shape themselves and I fasten them over
    my portal.
Their grinning ribs are stiff, as are their frozen lips
    (as worms are frozen by the sun).
The vault above the altar lifts me, melted, and
    paints my pillars with deadly sins.
My capitals are bitten with my own corrosion.
My body watches me.
Thus I serve my murdered shepherd, crooking the
    heads of hell and sucking their brittle blood.
They are so hot my hands are glass.
My lungs are caked with the wind they break.
When my body dies at last and shatters on the
    flags, and my ember bud ascends, I will leave
    the legions steaming in the stone.
You are neither mortal nor alone.
You are unwelcome in my walls.

Another Poetess

She stands to piss, then,
realizing her mistake, waits,
for instructions from her neighbors.

Her overpraised work was nothing so brittle
as all that. Naked sugar on the table
near the jar of water for her tea
turns brown with disuse. Murmurs of conversation
drift through the walls.

She weighs and considers the evidence,
then acts and re-acts
behind the howl of a poem.

Water

Are you still a sycophant,
on your knees, writing for profit?
You can't take your eyes
off your name. Even Narcissus
would rather sink than swim.

Dear ASPCA

Why can't I
get petted
or picked up
or stroked
or walked
or let in
or chased
or leashed
or bred
or mounted
or humped

Poem

It's not me
you see
sputtering
all over
it's not me
with something wrong
for a face
it's not me
you can't help
not to look at
it's not me

Commission

"Then write," she said. "By all means, if that's
    how you feel about it. Write poems.
Write about the recurved arcs of my breasts
    joined in an angle at my nipples, how
the upper arc tilts toward the sky and the lower
    reverses sharply back into my torso,
write about how my throat rises from the supple
    hinge of my collarbones proudly so to speak
with the coin-sized hollow at the center, write
    of the perfect arch of my jaw when I hold
my head back—these are the things in which I too
    take delight—write how my skin is
fine like a cover of snow but warm and soft and
    fitted to me perfectly, write the *volupté*
of soap frothing in my lovely crotch-hair, write
    the tight parabola of my vulva that re-
sembles a braided loop swung from a point,
    write the two dapples of light on the backs
of my knees, write my ankles so neatly turning
    in their sockets to deploy all the sweet
bones of my feet, write how when I am aroused
    I sway like a cobra and make sounds
of sucking with my mouth and brush my nipples
    with the tips of my left-hand fingers, and then
write how all this is continually pre-existing in my
    thought and how I effect it in myself
by my will, which you are not permitted to under-
    stand. Do this. Do it in pleasure and with
devotion, and don't worry about time. I won't
    need what you've done until you finish."

PLEASE SEND COUPON

AND PAYMENT INFORMATION TO:

THE QUARTERLY

SUBSCRIPTION DEPARTMENT

VINTAGE BOOKS

TWENTY-EIGHTH FLOOR

201 EAST 50TH STREET

NEW YORK, NY 10022

See last page to order back numbers.

Herewith payment or credit card information for the next four issues of *The Quarterly*.

Name_____

Address_____

City_____ State_____ Zip_____

_____ Enclosed is my check or money order for
      $40.00 ($54.00 in Canada)**, made out to
      Random House, Inc.

_____ Please charge my account with

American Express_____ MasterCard_____ Visa_____

Account # [   ]

Signature_____ Exp.____/
                                              mo. yr.

Inasmuch as *The Q* appears every three
months—namely, March, June, September,
December—please be patient for your
subscription to begin.

Strange but True

We were helpless, caught
in a vortex of water
72 miles in diameter.

Both my legs were broken,
but I still knew the meaning of the word
    "intermittent."

It was 1964.
1974.
Partly sunny.
Nobody was really sure.

Tomorrow was just a theory.

I asked her how she was getting home.
She said, "By water ambulance."

Love

I saw love once.
At first I thought it was a possum,
but then I realized it was not a possum.
It was love.
It was love lying there in the road.
My wife was with me at the time.
You can imagine how embarrassing it was.
Neither of us said anything at first.
What could we possibly have said?

We just drove on.
"Did you see that possum?" I asked.
But she would have no part of it.

Nobody Move

Something horrible is about to happen.
Then came World War II.
It had a good beat and was easy to dance to.

Nobody wants to do anything great anymore.

Ode on Ennui

The sun goes up,
the sun goes down.
The days pass like stones.

The Devil runs out of rotten things to do.

God sits in a waiting room,
waiting for the film to begin.

I'm looking for a b-word.

Beowulf, mortally wounded, drags himself into a
     cave.

He thinks: If I were a spider,
I would know what to do.

The Hands of Absence

Sitting in this measled light
of Christmas, where telephones
spin their combinations
in the dark, and ghosts
wash over my armchair.
One night, hunkered down
among old clothes, I slept
inside a St. Vincent
de Paul box. I scraped my name
into its belly
with a key I had found
in someone's pocket,
so many arms and legs
wrapped around me, so many bodies
blown down alleys
like leaves, or gone to God.

for John Woods

St. Jude's Home for Delinquent Boys

At night skyscrapers
throw down their nets
of light, drop coins
into the palms of drunks
who feel toward the sky for rain.

If I rubbed this night
over my skin, pieces of the moon
would rise and glisten,
like the scales of a smallmouth
as it leaps from the river.

Earlier, a naked boy
crawled by beneath my window,
slapping a trail of playing cards
facedown along the pavement.

I imagined myself leaping
through my bedroom window
as if into a strange painting,
wood silvers bristling
along my neck and back,
like the ruff on a
chained wolf-hound.

Metaphor on a Roadside Kill

Imagine it, pedestrians
all over America
lunging onto country roads,
antlers mounted to their heads.

They'd end up cartoon-flat
against the grilles of Mack trucks,
or twisted into a strange alphabet
of dangling tongues and twitching hands.

I want to say guts
strained out
through buttonholes of flesh,
or eyeballs rolling like coins
toward high weeds and ditches.

This ain't no Oz, man,
where you can stuff back in
that ooze. Grab a shovel-
sized spoon. In this country
we gorge on change.

JOHN RYBICKI

The Red Squirrel

It used to clatter around so
I'd jerk awake,
thinking rat, feeling rat
paws all over my skin.

Then a carpenter came,
corked his porthole out
with insulation, nailed
a wooden shingle over it.

All day I rev
ancient tractors, bobcat past
the heifer pens.

At night my bones arc out,
frame into a house,
where squirrels chase
along the wires of my arteries,
duck in and out
of my heart between the beats.

Yaakov Ben Nirriti

All night I struggled against him.
All night I dodged his plunging blade
    and parried with one arm
the certainty that he was God.
With the other I defeated
each one of his attempts to flee
    before he spoke a word
or lowered himself to bless me.

When he did, I saw the mask drop
for the first time and no longer
    knew what name to call him.
Laughing, I watched him touch my hip,
pressing till the socket shattered
    and I blacked out. I came

to in the tent, gasping between
the wives, and left with only pain.

The White Bull

He came out of the sea, stronger
and more comely than Poseidon,
    his brushed flanks finer than
Pegasus', his peg no stranger

to violent rut. The longer
I watched him tear the sand and turn
    his heavy head to one
side and another (the hunger

feeding his call), the more I saw
    how I could brace my thighs
and cant forward in Daedalus' cow,
    mute in her moony face,
eager to serve the god and bear—
to my husband's shame—Crete's savior.

The Bowdler Anthology of Late-Twentieth-Century Verse

Cooper Esteban (1953–   )

No less a critic than Steingebirge has complained, "Esteban has consistently utilized his not inconsiderable skills with traditional forms in the service of a petulant disdain for virtually all phenomenal existence. The juvenile, and relatively shallow, nature of his decadence reveals itself, even to the casual reader, through Esteban's diction—a flashy commingling of Latinate polysyllabics and street vulgarity" (*The New Review*, vol. 17, p. 1066). While Steingebirge is by no means alone in this conviction, there is another, possibly growing, camp. Most recently, Munir has offered, in Esteban's defense, a single quoted line—"the fallen light, the packed earth floor of the shed" (*English in Texas*, vol. 10, p. 20).

Four Calls from the Cleaners

Hare row? Itch itch Sung Lee wish
onehourmartinice. You half toupee
pant, two shut, and two tie.
You peacock for Monday, we fro way.
Ire pea—you half toupee pant, two shut,
and two tie. You peacock for Monday,
we fro way. Ire pea, we fro way.

Hare row? Itch itch Sung Lee wish
onehourmartinice. I caw and I caw
and I caw. You not heal me?
You knee phone wall round wish you.
Coalish! You knee coalish!
You not heal me? You knee coalish!

Hare row? Itch lash dime I caw.
You heal me? You half die clean you
knee peacock! You peacock for
Monday, we fro way! We fro way!

Itch itch Sung Lee.
You not evil heal me.
You knee coalish.
We fro way.
You heal me?

Jim Beats Off to Jane

See Jane fuck. Fuck, fuck, fuck.
Jane fucks Dick. Dick fucks Sue. Sue
fucks Jack. Jack fucks Mary. Mary fucks
Dick. Dick fucks Jane *and* Mary. Mary and
Jane fuck.
Time. It passes.
Jane fucks Time. Tim fucks Sally who
fucks Bob who fucks Joan who fucks Robert
who fucks Bob. Bob fucks Jane. Jane *sucks*
Jack. Jack, jack, jack. Jane fucks Spot,
a dog, for video. Spot fucks legs, pillows,
other dogs.
Dark and stormy nights pass.
Sue dies. Jack dies. Mary dies. Tim
dies.
Time, time, time.
Robert dies. Sally dies. Bob dies.
Joan moves to Greece, then dies. Dick dies.
Jane fucks Jim at the funeral party.
Getting close to the end of time. Jim
beats off to Jane on video with Spot.

Overheard

China
oh it's horrible
what's going on
you know
I've been
there

The Canal

Remembering is an old canal;
what used to connect one body to another
is now full of humidity and darkness,
and its granite walls are mortared
with lichen and moss.

I remember how we crossed
a long wooden bridge.
Upstream, the state had planted
steel girders to stop trees and debris
from toppling the bridge.
The girders grow proud
with rust and wreckage.

Father,
When I finally reached the water
I stood on the stone landing
and listened to fish break the surface.
You told me they would feed on anything, even
stones and seeds if that's all you had.
I kicked in some dust,
and watched a school of shadows move in.

The Denizen

I'm embarrassed to admit it:
the men who truck the trash
away on Tuesday mornings
have become my favorite friends.
Harry and Dil—they know my name.
We laughed at the head
of my ex-lover. Harry dropped it
or it broke through the bag all by itself;
we don't like to argue. Anyhow,
the head lay on the pavement.
Dil grabbed it by the hair
and held it high, his other grip
on an invisible hilt at his hip,
and said he was Hercules.
Harry agreed. We argued until
I got a book from the house
and proved Dil was Perseus.
They'd never heard of Perseus,
the stupid fucks. I said
I might wind up in trouble
if someone saw Dil
waving the head around.
Harry and Dil agreed and said
they had better be getting
back to their route anyway,
and Dil pitched the head and trash
into the stinking truck.

           The air was warm,
so I waited on the porch to have
a few words with the paperboy.

He'd flung the Monday edition
into my petunia bed and I desired
to shake my fist at him until
his tender lips quivered.

We talked for hours. He helped me
clip coupons and ate my
leftover spaghetti. We discussed
the bent petunias
like reasonable human beings
until the beer got to his head
and made him wise.

Learning to Forget

I am trapped by the naming of things;
heal-alls, crown vetch, snake lilies.
Grown in the bark of the woods,
jack pine, pawpaw, pin oak, ash.
Stones underfoot hold their names
like tiny fossils, shale, flint.

In a grove of locust trees, I settle
among beds of flattened timothy
pulsing with the ghosts of deer. The sun
slips delicately through thorns
above me. I close my eyes and listen
to a starling call in the distance
from a tree I cannot see, cannot name.

The Rain House

I think soon the soldiers will come
and snatch the potatoes from the babies,
send them off to night school to learn Latin.
If I could think a clear thought,
I would,
but
the Speaker's heart is sinking like
a diamond in milk
and his friends are all boarding the plane.

There is a report on page three of the newspaper
that Mr. Wright is in trouble.
I don't doubt it.

There are many roads out of
Grand Prairie.
Tomorrow the Speaker will be having lunch
at the Ridgelea Country Club,
a carnation in his lucky lapel.

Then he will fly back to Washington where
the cherry blossoms
are weeping along the wandering, steady Potomac.

As usual,
Betty will be at his side.

Effortless

The Circle K

Cliff and I drive the baby across the desert to visit his grandma in Utah. We pick up a man on the desert. He just needs to stop at the Circle K. He's going to Utah, like us, but we can leave him in Page, he says, he's got some friends there. Hasn't Cliff seen him around the town where we live sometimes? Probably, the man says. After Page, I fall asleep. In my dream it is snowing. In the dream we are already at my mother's house. But we don't go in. We just sit in the car and wait. Then I wake up. The baby is sleeping. Cliff is playing some tapes on his little tape recorder, mostly country. There are empty baggies on the seat, from the chicken I made for the trip. I get them up. It is dark now. I see the lost are like this.

Given by Joe

Eleanor had a small red pocketbook given to her on her seventh birthday by a man named Joe. Related to her how? Eleanor did not know.

It was the best gift given. It was like, Eleanor thought, there was some sort of quota and she was only allowed one good gift a year. Eleanor liked to keep the pocket-book near.

Inside it she kept: her mother's coral lipstick, the shade she no longer wore, several important phone numbers and a small container that could hold quarters if she wanted. Eleanor had memorized the things in her purse. She liked the way they looked. She did not want them to change.

On the Bus

I set
The tennis ball
Between my feet
When the bus slows down
It rolls
To the front
Two high-school girls
Giggle
Kick it
The bus speeds up
The ball
Comes rolling
Back

Traveling

As it happened, he was writing,
and I could see Paris,
New York, London, L.A.
penned into squares of week
after week, and I knew
he sat on planes all the time
and never looked at the woman
sitting next to him, never had to,
just wrote cities into his book
with those hands to make her think of places
she wants to be taken by a man
who knows every place;
she watches him make those notes
and she takes out her lipstick
and runs it, red and
smooth and moist around her
mouth, parted like an answer.

Helpless

For years
we pushed his wheelchair everywhere.
Last week
he stood up and walked out
to the car.
We have not seen the bastard
since.

Philodendron

I wanted one thing alive
to keep me company in the bare
apartment so you sent me
a philodendron, saying
nothing I could fail to do
would kill it.

I put it on the heating
unit, which kept it warm
in winter, air-conditioned
in summer, gave it a cup
of water daily, never
bothered to prune it.

It grew magnificently.
I watched axils open,
bracts and spathes multiply,
spadices appear day
after day, week by month.
It ran around one corner

of the room, behind
the TV, along a bookcase,
up and then over
the patio window.
Before you moved in
I'd named it

Pheidippides, for the
Athenian runner who
delivered his message

to Sparta before he fell
during the reign
of Xerxes, King of Persia.

We posed you like a goddess,
the twenty-six feet of it
draped over your out-
stretched arms, wound
around your body and legs,
curled like a crown

on your head. We thought
it would never die.
Then, one day, we noticed
how sad it somehow seemed—
and overreacted. We gave
it more water, moved it,

tried stimulants, everything
we could think of. Daily
we cut the dead away,
tried to get new shoots
to grow in water. All
to no avail. One morning

the final foot of it
lay so yellow and withered
we knew there was
nothing more we could do.
How well I remember
the day we threw it away.

We came back up from the South about 2 weeks ago and got back here to Poplar Bluff for the family reunion, which was an experience Not To Be Missed, what with 4 of us women cousins ending up sitting in a van at 1:30 A.M. drinking beer and telling stories about my daddy and Uncle Darwin. God, we laughed & then kind of ended up weeping about Aunt Pete's suicide & Aunt Dickie's death (they were the twins). The family is so close. Hard to describe. People grow up so damn poor— all they got is each other. After the family reunion, Susan-Marie & Mark & me went over to Eminence with the horses, where it rained buckets & bathtubs for 5 days straight, & Susan's new horse lamed up and, if you can believe this—here I am by myself and Jim is clear across the damn state to take the motor home to be repaired there where he bought it. Also, he is back over there where he can get in some good fights with his ex-wife over property and stuff. Jim enjoys a good fight. You should have seen us at Eminence. Soon as we got there, we tried to ride Susan's big Appaloosa double & the meathead bucked me off, and I started crying, & told Jim he cared more about fighting with his ex-wife and his recalcitrant daughters than being in love with me, and he said, You bet, honey, that's how come I bought that goddamned motor home & drove us all the way to the Florida Keys, looking for your cousins, and so forth and so on, & about then was when that Appaloosa started bucking its way across the camp & sending people scattering, & then I fell off. And Jim sat in the motor home & got quietly & stubbornly drunk as only a Texan can, & I got so mad at him, I cut my hair off short with the cooking scissors. But we're too old to get in these kinds of fights, so we quit, and got dressed up and went to the dance. It was amazing, all these people out doing the Cotton-Eye & Texas 9-Step in the rain

& mud. At these outdoor dances, people back their pickups up to the dance floor so they can sit up in the pickup beds in lawn chairs & drink beer & soda out of coolers & watch the dancing. So these cowpokes were out dancing in their hats and cattle dusters down to their ankles. The cattle dusters are very graceful to dance in. They drift out around ankles & legs as you move around. Shed rain, too—shed it right down onto spurs. Anyway, Eminence was a bust; it was like living thru a monsoon. There were some people out riding in the rain, but there are always crazy people in a crowd of 2000 or over. By Friday, they were having to get out tractors & other heavy machinery to pull horse trailers & other rigs out of the mud, & the Jack's Fork River was up to the banks. Mark & Susan-Marie took the van to go up to St. Louis to get their kids where they'd left them with our cousins Robbie Lynn & Judy. To mollify family, I went to interview Aunt Byatt because she's the oldest of the living aunts. Aunt Byatt talks to Elvis Presley on the Ouija board and says Spaniards left all this gold at the bottom of the Black River, etc. Well, what's happening now is I can't wait to settle down in one place and have everything be regular. That's the reward in life I am looking for right now, me and Jim to have a place where we can cook Mexican breakfasts and look out the window & see the same stuff for a month at a time. I am missing Jim so much, I could just pack up & leave now. Here's a camp meeting notice. Doniphan is just over the way from here. I hope they save a lot of people from the devil & from Ouija boards.

We have been here on St. Simon's now three weeks because this criminal in Tampa has been holding the pickup, promising day after day they would have it done. Gibsonton, just at the south edge of Tampa, is where all the circus and carnival people winter & turns out this guy supposedly repairing the pickup (*"You Bend 'Em, We Mend 'Em"*) is a carny type. Jim flew down on Monday to pick it up because they said for sure it was done & when he arrived it wasn't & they wanted $1,000 *more* over and above the insurance, but the insurance

ANNUAL
BIBLE WAY ASSOCIATION

1989   1989

CAMP MEETING

MON. JUNE 19 THRU SAT. JUNE 24

Bible Way Camp Grounds

3½ Miles West Of Doniphan, Missouri On Highway 160

THREE SERVICES DAILY:

10:00 a.m. — Teaching & Preaching —
2:00 p.m. — Special Preaching Services
7:30 p.m. — Old Time Camp Meeting Services —

SPEAKERS: Leslie Buckner, Charles Asberry, Roy Scates and various other
Bible Way Association ministers.

CAMPGROUND FACILITIES:

★ **Restrooms
and Showers**

**Hookups
For Campers**

Rooms will be available at the campground on a
first-come-first-served basis. (Bring your own bedding.)
    You may choose a room in town (at your own
expense). Contact Hillview Motel, Ph. 996-2101,
or North End Motel, Ph. 996-2164.
* Freewill offering basis
* Everyone is welcome regardless of affiliation
* Dorms, cabins, trailer hookups, tent sites,
  plenty of shower rooms, sewer hookups
* Large dining hall - two meals served each day
  on a freewill offering basis

**BREAKFAST & SUPPER
SERVED DAILY**

**Bring Tents,
Bedding,**

"COME AND SPEND THE WEEK"

Everyone Welcome

guy came to Jim's rescue & went out with him to the shop ("*You Stall 'Em, We Haul 'Em*") so they wouldn't have the total advantage over a lone traveler—but down there in all the junky car and body-repair places are lots full of concession carts (POPCORN! COTTON CANDY! etc.) parked for the winter & a retirement home for wild animals who are old. Jim saw an old, old elephant strolling across a lawn at a WILD ANIMAL RETIREMENT PARK, kind of crippling along. Anyhow, he paid the guy $700 extra & got out of there after an argument & it wasn't until Jim was on the road back here to St. Simon's that he noticed the guy hadn't even put the rearview mirror back on, & that he had stolen the rear wheel-slings and the wheel-lock device for the steering wheel, and notices also, on the price list, that the guy has charged him $65 to cut a new ignition key. And so on and so on and so on. But as to wine and roses, we were having some truly gruesome fights & when I started one the last time I think Jim decided instead of yelling & shouting to be kind & patient & understanding & etc., & so I didn't have anybody to blame for all my bad behavior, and then Jim had to stay 3 days in Tampa, & so I had time to think about this, and made some major decisions about not pouting or losing my temper—like I don't want to end up in a WILD ANIMAL RETIREMENT HOME. So the lieutenant colonel & myself are as blissful as we were in Montana, or more so. Did I tell you he & 2 other LC's rewrote the Army doctrine on guerrilla warfare? And so tonight I went over to the bathhouse here at this RV park, & the woman in the shower next to me w/2 little ones is saying (after "Where y'all from?") as she scrubbed these two little girls, "Yeah, me & Kirk, you know, he's an electrician on at the X Construction Company here at Dublin (Georgia) and last time he was on a crew I spent 9 months at home in West Virginia alone, &, man, I tell you, these two kids come down with strep throat & chicken pox all within a week of each other, & I call Kirk & I say, 'Kirk, I cain't do this alone, honey,' & he said, 'Well, babe, what you gonna do?' & I said, 'Well, I tell you what, I'm buying a camper & I'm coming down there.' So we're all living in this little camper & these girls look like somebody beat on 'em, running around & playing & falling down & getting mosquito-bit, but I tell you, next to living alone, there w/2 little kids in West Virginia, we're in tall cotton!"

We started out from St. Simon's this A.M. from Jim's brother's place where we've been camping on Bubba for three weeks & got 3 miles down the road & the trailer broke down again—Jim's been using 2 come-alongs to hold the pickup to the trailer instead of the slings—the slings the shop ("You Lose 'Em, We Rob 'Em") stole, & nearly lost the lot—but Jim & a cop & a helpful kid got the thing rehooked up, & we went on. This trip is the best thing that ever happened to me. I been ouching a little. But I met the person I was meant to share my life with. And so Jim & Bubba got a letter from their mama in Houston while we were there, and she starts off, "Hi. It is May 18, 1989, 1:00 A.M., I am up waiting for the tornado to hit." and ends, "There was an article in the paper saying there was a small killer shark in the Trinity River." I have been staying in close contact with my sis Sunny in St. Louis. I cooked meat-loaf tonight in the little oven, & on the road between Macon & Savannah I got out the guitar & Jim and I sang "Darling Nelly Gray" and "You Are My Sunshine," and I wrote down the names of rivers—& swamps—& we shut it all up tonight & turned on the air conditioning. **Q**

Do you ever miss what goes on in magazine offices? Yesterday some television technicians were here because we are doing a cover story on whatever became of the hippies who went to Woodstock twenty years ago. Our famous photographs of these hippies, some with little or no clothing, were pinned onto the cork walls, and one of the cameramen took close-ups. The editor and the art director discussed which pictures ought to be used in the magazine, and everyone looked uncomfortable under the bright lights. You can watch it all on one of those Sunday-morning shows. We do these things because we think it will cause television viewers to say, "Hey, I'm going to buy that magazine and really study those hippies frolicking in the mud with little or no clothing on." The television people do it because they have vast periods of time to fill and, since they just had to walk across the street to shoot this tape, this is a cheap way to take note of an important event in America's recent past. While the television technicians were packing up their gear, the young staff members headed off to Central Park to play softball against a team from another major American magazine. I took the opportunity to leave the office nine minutes earlier than usual. On the train I got out my pen and paper and wrote this down to serve as a kind of document of something that happened on June 21, 1989.

When I got home, I drank a bourbon, ate beef hash, and then went to the basement to work on a wooden cat I'm making with two mice inside playing a game of checkers. When I finish it, I will send it to a company in San Francisco that will ship it to Sri Lanka where craftsmen will make two hundred copies. **Q**

In a family, nothing is more surprising and life-renewing than the return in a new context of an event thought at first to be singular. In their cumulative effect such returns reach mysteriously both ahead and back in time, so that, however particular the time and place of an event, one may be both elsewhere and home. But all this must be proven on one's pulses as one begins the risky, repetitive, continually surprising, and always mysterious enterprise of family living. And so in due time I am trying desperately to finish a book review as my wife's vital contractions accelerate. Suddenly it is time, she hurries to the kitchen sink to shampoo her hair, I stop in mid-paragraph and hurry her to the hospital where soon our second daughter is born. Without the omniscience of the plot-controlling novelist, I am unable to foresee that many years later that daughter will be with us in Paris. She will rise early in our Left Bank bed-and-breakfast quarters to go running and I will lie there with the joyous picture of her taking her favorite route: up Rue Bonaparte to the Seine, down to Pont St. Michel and across it to circle Notre Dame, over to the Right Bank and down to the Louvre, then home by way of Pont Royal. In the time constraints of the family plot, however, I can only flash-back to our honeymoon in the conventional lakeside cottage—where, because of the primitive accommodations, my bride must wash her beautiful hair in the lake and I am able to watch her from a cabin window as she kneels on the edge of the dock. But both shampooings are preparing me to think badly of the man we will ultimately meet in St. Peter's Square in Rome two days after the Pope has been shot, we being there in part for a family reason: to stand on the roof of the basilica and take pictures from the same spot where our grand-touring first daughter once stood. The man is with his wife and he is still angry. They had come down from Germany the day before the historic event and the wife, overdue for a shampoo and hairdo, made an appointment with a hairdresser so that they arrived in the square an hour too late for the shooting. My sympathies are with the wife, who looks nice, if somewhat chastened, with her fresh hairdo. Hadn't she only wanted to look nice for her husband, and perhaps for the Pope as well—just as my shampooing wife had wanted to look nice for me?

Repetitions in good novels are incremental just as they are in medieval ballads, where the repetition of verses in changing contexts carries the plot ahead. Thus in *The Great Gatsby* the repetition of moments that articulate a discovery of illusion after glorious expectation build up incrementally to that final moment when the reader is elsewhere with those long-ago Dutch sailors who in a "transitory enchanted moment" behold the "fresh, green breast of the new world," never dreaming how far it will fall short of its promise. But the plot of a family, too, is structured with the incremental repetitions of secular and sacred rituals that dramatize the unspoken conviction that the failure to celebrate a recurring event is an implicit judgment that it was worthless to begin with. In vital families the celebration of each baptism and birthday is separate and special and yet has been enrichingly prepared for by the celebration of all previous baptisms and birthdays. The eggs are colored each Easter Eve in the same basement room at the same time, but the children, like developing writers, refine their techniques and come up with novel effects. And each family has its own ritual style, its own way of vitalizing its identifying plot. Families that have lost, or never had, the capacity for plot-sustaining innovations are condemned like the victims of autism to repetition without increment, which is the fate of those lost souls who people Dante's *Inferno*. Even apparently disastrous interruptions of the familiar ritual pattern may, as in novels, turn out to be memorable surprises. Thus on the eve of a Sunday confirmation the car breaks down and we must hire two taxis to get everyone to the church and back for the celebratory breakfast afterward. The children, excited with their first taxi ride, obviously think that the failure of the family car has made their day.

The family picnic, like Christmas one of the most incrementally repetitious of rituals, is one of the best ways to be at once elsewhere and home, which is why the better the picnic, the more everyone enjoys being home again. So after the children have gone off to establish their own separate yet interconnected lives, the picnic *à deux* continues to be a family affair. We are, for instance, at Versailles in mid-May, early picnic time at home. We buy ham sandwiches and cans of Coke at a stand near the Fountain of Latina and go down where the white blossoms of the great chestnut trees are tossing like pompoms in the light midday wind. As we eat we can see a corner of the Petit Trianon where the randy Louis XV had once enjoyed the favors of Madame Du Barry, doomed many years later to die on the guillotine. There is a tree-nestled honeymoon privacy about the place that takes me back to the much less opulent privacy of our own honeymoon cabin in the pines. The latter becomes the destination of a family picnic, the aim being to show the children their true beginnings and at the same time grill hamburgers on a new charcoal burner. The children are respectful enough but hardly overwhelmed. Like the readers of *The Great Gatsby* who encounter for the first time the valley of ashes between West Egg and Manhattan, they must take on faith that the place will ultimately prove to be a significant elsewhere in the family plot. Later on the beach they are more impressed with the improvement of hot hamburgers over previous picnic fare.

But for my wife and I it is a Proustian return, and I remember our long honeymoon walk on a golden August afternoon, down the narrow dirt road that runs past the cabin and out into pastoral farmland. We are living for the moment, dispensed from historical time like Fitzgerald's Dutch sailors, not knowing that the walk is prologue to an incremental repetition of elsewhere walks. Thus we are at Giverny in France on another golden afternoon in order to see Claude Monet's watery pastoral domain. It is easy to imagine the artist at work in his studio there, smoking his daily forty cigarettes in the domestic silence he insisted on, but there is little sense of family left, though as modern painters go he was, like his friend Matisse, a better than average family man. When we have had our fill of his water lilies and Japanese prints we walk down a country road that Monet would have known well, but we are no longer thinking of him. He has said of his work: "The subject is of secondary importance to me; what I want to reproduce is what exists between the subject and me." He has become of secondary importance to us. What we will reproduce later is not Monet but the repeated timelessness of that walk on a pastoral afternoon.

Or we are at Kildare in Ireland walking down a fairy-story country lane through hay-sweet horse fields, having no other objective after the exciting noise of Paris, London, and Dublin than living for an hour or two in a dispensation of green silence. We come to the bone-white remnant of a castle, stoop to enter its trash-littered keep. It is open like a giant chimney so that we can see birds wheeling far above us in the silver satin sky, and we know that if our sons were with us they would find some way to climb up there and scare us to death. Or we are in Venice having left St. Mark's and crossed the Grand Canal by the Rialto bridge to go honeymoon walking by narrow winding ways and across murky and rotten-smelling small canals till we are pleasantly lost—unlike that doomed bachelor Gustave Aschenbach, who, after a similar excursion in pursuit of his beloved Tadzio in Thomas Mann's *Death in Venice,* ends up miserably distraught. We come to a small café where we get excellent white wine and sit outside drinking it a stone's throw from a soccer-loud schoolyard. The players are caught up like honeymooners in their mysterious elsewhere, and they send me synchronically back to another schoolyard to which I have been called because our eldest son has been injured in a pickup football game during afternoon recess. I must return him, fortunately not for long, to the hospital where he was born.

In the developing family plot there are no elsewheres of pure escape, just as in Melville's great novel there is no place where Moby Dick is not present. So we are in New York, returning along Fifty-fifth Street after a visit to the UN, and note that something is happening at the Third Avenue intersection. A man in a drab black suit hurries past us, extracting something from a pocket of his jacket. It is a purple stole. At the intersection two police cars have halted the impatiently honking traffic, a city bus has pulled up at an odd angle, someone covered by a yellow tarp is lying beside it and the priest is there reading from a small black book. A bystander tells us that the victim was a young bicycle rider whose head had been crushed by a back wheel of the bus. The corner of the tarp keeps flapping up and the stalled traffic keeps on honking. There is nothing to do but walk on, carrying the image of our second son lying on a curbing beside stalled traffic. I have been summoned from home by one of the other children. He lies there quiet as death, his face drained of color. He had been riding his bike on the wrong side of the street, crashed head-on into an auto, and ended up sprawled on the hood. The bike is a twisted ruin. As I bend over him, his eyes open. An ambulance arrives and again it is off to the hospital, by now the most familiar of elsewheres.

I will soon learn that he is only badly shaken-up—but as I await the verdict, I am sitting in the same room I had occupied a year before as I waited to learn whether our third son had broken his arm. He has fallen from the kitchen countertop in the process of trying to steal cookies from an upper cupboard and I have been called off the golf course to rush him to the hospital. So in the family plot, incremental repetitions can go backward as well as forward in that suspension of chronological sequence that Forster so admires in novels.

Members of families have always known this, at least existentially. Once novelists learned to imitate the experience of time in families, novels have never been the same.

This fact, however, has not kept modern novelists (to say nothing of counterculture gurus like the British psychiatrist R. D. Laing) from doing their part to publicize the family as an institution uncongenial to artistic personalities. A proper place to remember this bias is in Forster's own Bloomsbury, an area that, thanks to the British Museum, the fine periodicals library of the University of London, and the Safeway supermarket, has always been one of the most agreeable of elsewhere for us. Bloomsbury, like all bohemias and countercultures, was an aesthetic enclave in which creativity and self-enhancement, not family nurturing, came first. From the perspective of such places, the more ideal or happy the family, the more its plot is a prison from which the creative individual must escape. This may be why family members like Hemingway or Joyce who are scheduled to become novelists act as though they need to justify their escape by making their families more unhappy than they might otherwise be. Perhaps they are motivated by an anticipatory fear that if a family could be as successfully plotted as a novel, it could not help being anti-novel. Most likely this fear was behind what his biographer P. N. Furbank called Forster's distrust of marriage as an institution and his irritation "at having to write 'marriage fiction.' " Only the work of art is supposed to be happy without crippling dependence on elsewheres outside itself. The happy family is its adversary, which may be why novelists and other artists tend to make such a mess of things when they get in a family way themselves.

But it would probably be better to speak of good rather than happy families: "happy" suggests an invulnerability to the happenstance of time. Good families are sometimes less than happy just as good novels are at some points less than good. Certainly there were moments when the Tolstoy family, thanks to the master's passionate eccentricities, was unhappy in its own way. Good families can survive the same vicissitudes that make other families bad. Like good novels, they depend on the strength of their commitment to well-chosen plots. Perhaps nothing is more likely to make a potentially good family unhappy and bad than the mistake of putting happiness first, as Tolstoy's Anna Karenina and Flaubert's Madame Bovary do. The analogous mistake for the novelist is his failure as he writes to keep out of his mind the need to so overwhelm his readers and critics that his self-doubts will be gone forever. In our culture, unfortunately, families, like individuals, can become so addicted to happiness that anything short of continual domestic euphoria is intolerable. Perhaps, then, families should be graded less by their degree of happiness than by their ability to stand up to the causes of unhappiness. Indeed, one of the functions of a good family plot is to teach the liberating lesson that it is possible to live purposefully, and even fulfillingly, without being always happy. A condition of uninterrupted happiness, in fact, would mean repetition without increment, and without mystery or surprise. Not having had a chance to learn this, Anna Karenina and Madame Bovary have no alternative but to sacrifice themselves to the well-being of their novels.

If a family can do without unalloyed happiness, it cannot do without the renewing power of those returns from elsewhere that celebrate its always mysterious and surprising existence in time. So we are at the airport awaiting our third daughter's return from a year's schooling in Florence. After she arrives, I am distracted for a moment, then turn to see that all three daughters have joined hands and are celebrating their reunion with a joyful dance. A few years later my wife and I are elsewhere again, in Florence now, visiting the room in the pension where that daughter lived during her great year abroad, and again I see my daughters dancing on the carpet of the concourse. In my mind they will never stop dancing. **Q**

TOM AHERN

You take the thing from its nest in the box and peel away the newspaper wrapping. It's a pottery candlestick the size and shape of a longshoreman's thumb, in dirty blues and grays, worth a dollar when it was new twenty years ago, and now, with inflation, worth maybe fifty cents, if cleaned up. The candle socket, too large for the candles that were available when it was used, is lined with aluminum foil several layers thick, and the space between the layers is filled with red wax or perhaps dark pink wax, looking not like blood but rather like melted lipstick. It's a thing your wife brought to the marriage, acquired probably during college days, with candlelit dinners in the back of her mind. Not to be snobbish about it, it's a thing you might have bought yourself in your college days, with candlelit dinners in the back of your mind.

You are preparing to take part in a giant citywide garage sale, held at the coliseum, where you will divest yourselves of dozens of items like this candlestick, which you have been carting around from apartment to apartment for decades, never used, unwanted, invisible in their newspaper wrappings—but not weightless, no, and not without bulk. You are cleaning out the closets, right down to the floor, by God, right back to the wallpaper.

It is primarily your task. This is because Marcia has a job, while you do not—at least not in the sense that it's a regular occupation, with regular hours and regular pay. You are a writer, she has a job. It's quite a taxing job she has, brings in the money that supports the two of you and so on—the writer's life, all that.

You have six boxes filled already. Three large rented tables will be waiting for you in your space at the coliseum. Your wife says, "Do we have enough stuff to fill three tables?" and you reply, "If we don't, we can go round and buy more from the other vendors."

You reach into the socket of the candlestick to pluck out the foil lining, but the foil lining does not pluck out. It doesn't even budge. You take it into the kitchen, where a single drawer holds all the tools an unhandy man needs to bang the occasional nail, screw the occasional screw, and gouge the occasional hole. The first that offers itself to your hand is an ordinary standard ratchet screwdriver with keystone tip, square shank, and fluted handle in transparent amber plastic. Not necessarily the right tool for the right job, but surely a tool capable of digging a wad of tinfoil out of a candlestick.

You work the tip in between the outermost layer of foil and the unglazed clay of the candlestick, and pry. This is a bit tricky, because the fulcrum of this action is the lip of the candlestick itself; therefore, you pry gently. Gentle prying has no effect at all; the circular wall of foil and wax remains unmoved. It seems necessary to reduce the thickness of the wall by stripping away some of its inner layers. You begin hacking at them with the screwdriver.

It isn't as though you're sponging on Marcia, or even imposing on her. If you foreswore writing and got a job, she would go on working anyway; the result would just be more money to throw around—not ultimately or deeply gratifying to either of you. The novel you're working on can wait, is used to waiting, in fact. You have the time to assemble the stuff for the sale and she doesn't.

These two substances, wax and aluminum foil, individually fragile, make a formidable armor when combined. The wax coats the foil and lends it gummy strength, and the foil clings to the wax like a malicious force of gravity, so the screwdriver can neither penetrate the foil nor claw away the wax. The Department of Defense should know of this material.

You set aside the screwdriver and delve in the tool drawer for your superior combination, or slip-joint, pliers, made of lustrous steel alloy, with handles dipped in nonslip red plastic.

With these, you begin to rip at the foil. It is not particularly your idea to rip at it, but that's what it amounts to—the inner liner cannot be parted from the candlestick as a whole; it will only come away in shreds. After a few minutes of labor, you succeed in chewing away the top quarter inch of the foil all around, leaving the rest behind, beyond the reach of your heavy-jawed pliers.

You see at last that you can only succeed if you penetrate and destroy the ground in which the foil is rooted. You return to the drawer and bring forth a tool suited to this task: a screwdriver with a Phillips head, a sixty-five millimeter blade, round shank, and fluted handle in clear plastic, with scarlet collar and deeply notched butt. You plunge the blade into the candlestick and feel it sink into the muck. You drag the point across the bottom but do not manage to disembowel the thing; in fact, you dredge up nothing but crumbs. You go back in again and again, a Jack the Ripper of candlesticks.

Does this rooting about in the unexamined baggage of your marriage have some deep, hidden significance? Is this garage sale in fact a parable of your lives? Are you sending a signal to each other that you need to conduct a *distress sale*? Is it perhaps an unconscious statement of marital bankruptcy? Are the two of you mindlessly preparing for some change neither is ready to discuss? Or even to think about?

Working over the sink, you see that it is collecting a litter of greasy crumbs. Will these crumbs clog the garbage disposal? Of course they will. These crumbs would clog a three-bottom plow, a nuclear reactor. As you take them to the trash, you see that, careful as you've been, the kitchen floor has likewise collected a litter of the crumbs, which, under the pressure of your feet, have doubtless bonded to the tile at the molecular level.

Tilting the candlestick to catch the light, you see that the bottom of the candle socket has been considerably churned up by your efforts. More, you see that you have fished up an old unburned wick, which lies there like the mummy of some obscene gray worm. You dig at it, but it effortlessly eludes the point of the Phillips screwdriver. It seems to you that the buried end of the wick must lie at the very bottom of the candlestick. It seems to you highly likely that, if you could just get hold of it, you could use this wick to hoick out the whole obstruction like a bathtub plug.

Can you reach it with the pliers? No. You would be able to reach it with needle-nose pliers, as used by jewelry-makers and electricians, or with duckbill pliers, as used by weavers and telephone workers, but not with your combination, or slip-joint, pliers, despite their superiority.

You can reach it with a finger, of course.

Exploring the rosy depths, you feel the wick squirt away from your touch like a tendon. You find that you can trap it against the rough wall of the candle socket with a fingernail, but this doesn't let you exert any useful pressure on it. You take the problem into the bathroom and attack it with a pair of zirconium tweezers. These tweezers are so beautifully engi-neered that you could lift a five-pound infant with them, given a toe to hold it by—but not if the toe was waxed. The wick glides through the perfectly aligned jaws of the tweezers like a tendril of smoke. You return to the kitchen and continue your efforts with the Phillips screwdriver.

On the whole, there is not much for either of you to resent in this marriage. You, for example, do not resent being sad-dled with this chore of getting ready for the garage sale. You have the time to do it, and Marcia does not. In the same way, you do not resent doing the shopping or the laundry or the dishes, even though these things naturally cut into the time you have to spend at the word processor. For her part, your wife has just as much not to resent. She does not resent your having perpetual access to a well-stocked refrigerator or to a sofa on which you may recline while having lunch and reading a novel. It is not necessary for her to refrain from resenting either your daytime tippling or your television watching, be-cause you are not tempted by either one, but there are plenty of other things for her not to resent. For example, she does not resent the fact that you may work or not, as you please and when you please, without anyone nagging or looking over your shoulder; she knows that—if they are like you—people who work when they please, without anyone nagging or looking over their shoulders, are so much eaten up with guilt that resenting them is quite gratuitous.

To your sudden amazement, you find you are no longer able to do any useful digging with the sixty-five millimeter blade of your Phillips screwdriver. It is as though the tip has broken through the space at the bottom of the candlestick and is now probing an abyss in some other galaxy. Luckily, there is a longer Phillips screwdriver in the tool drawer, one with a round shank, a black wooden handle, and a pink rubber grip with alternating plain and scored panels.

You gather up the wax crumbs that have accumulated in the sink and transfer them to the trash.

You estimate that by now you have spent twenty minutes trying to clean a candlestick you intend to price at fifty cents. You imagine someone at the garage sale—a young man, perhaps—picking it up, giving it a brief, contemptuous examination, and asking, "Will you take a quarter for it?"

A *quarter*? You shake your head, insulted.

Thirty-five cents?

You turn away to hide your disgust.

Angling the thing to catch the light, you see that the foil and wax have been chewed, chopped, scraped, and dug away to a depth of two inches below the lip of the candlestick. Miraculously, there is still more of the muck down there. A full inch of that obscene, pale wick has been exposed; it lies in the rubble, beaten limp by the fury of your onslaught.

You unleash upon it the additional fifteen millimeters of your new weapon.

Marcia has no secretary, so you cannot wonder if she is having an affair with him. You can, however, plausibly wonder: Is she thinking of leaving you? Financially, it would make sense; it must be a temptation for her. On the other hand, do working husbands think of leaving their housebound wives just because it would be cheaper to live without them? Of course not. Or at least not ordinarily.

Would you bleat like an abandoned housewife: *Oh, but what is to become of me? How will I live?*

Would she think it a responsibility to look after you until you got on your feet?

Under your attack, something has at last broken loose in the depths of the candlestick. You think it is its heart.

Yes. You can see it now. A walnut of pink wax, sprouting the unburned wick, has been broken loose from the surrounding walls. Incredibly, the candle socket *widens* at the bottom, forming a little dungeon that holds this plug of wax back. You can rotate it in the dungeon with the point of your screwdriver, but you cannot free it. It must be split, cut to pieces, before it can be liberated.

Is this a metaphor for something?

You hold the plug of wax in place with the point of the screwdriver. You hold it, readying yourself. Then you stab. The plug spins in the socket. You haven't even nicked it.

Once again you pin the plug of wax in place with the screwdriver. Once again you hold it, readying yourself. Once again you stab. Once again the plug spins in the socket.

Surely this is a metaphor for something. Life. Marriage. Something.

You try again, and again the plug spins in the socket.

You have a feverish sort of inspiration. You hold the candlestick under the faucet and fill it with water, but the plug does not comply with the inspiration; it does not float up out of its dungeon.

The young man of your imagination picks it up, turns it this way and that, and asks, "Will you take a quarter for it?"

Turning your head away to conceal your bitterness, you hold out a hand for the quarter.

You empty the water, attack again with the screwdriver,

and are not surprised to discover that wet wax is even more slippery than dry wax. For all you're accomplishing, you might as well be stabbing a tempered-steel ball bearing with a swizzlestick.

There is only one thing to be done. The plug of wax must be crushed.

Crushed, by God!

This is not impossible. No, not impossible.

Using the side of the screwdriver blade, you press the plug against the wall of its dungeon. Yes. Now you are ready. But you must be gentle, for once again you are using the lip of the candlestick as the fulcrum for your lever. You increase the pressure against the plug of wax, little by little building up to a crushing force.

The plug rolls in the socket, sliding away.

You must try again. There is now no other way. The plug must be crushed and the fragments drawn up out of the dungeon like . . . like . . . fragments.

Once again you force the plug up against the wall. Once again you center the blade of the screwdriver against the bulbous waist. Is it centered? Is it stable? Does it grip this goddamned motherplugger like a swivel eye gripping the slotted flap of a brushed-brass hasp?

It is, by God. It is and it does.

With the hand of a patient gorilla, you draw back on the screwdriver. You draw back on the screwdriver, exerting on that plug the sort of force that exists in the center of collapsing stars, the sort of force that mashes atoms, the sort of force that—

With an astonishing violence and suddenness, the candlestick explodes in your hands, spattering your glasses with dots of water and spraying gobbets of wax and pottery everywhere. When everything has landed and settled, the uncrushable wax plug sits in the drain of the sink like a maraschino cherry, shiny and intact. There is an ugly, painful gash in the palm of your hand where you dragged the point of the screwdriver through it. The gash is bleeding well—very well. You need not waste any time worrying whether this cut is bleeding well. You hold it under the cold water tap until the wound begins to bleed somewhat less well—then you carry it, cushioned in a paper towel, to the bathroom, where you cover it with a sterile adhesive bandage with nonstick pad and unique, long-lasting adhesive. While you're there, you rinse off the zirconium tweezers and return them to their snug felt holster.

The kitchen gives you something to sigh about. There is blood and water everywhere. There are gobbets of wax and shards of pottery everywhere. You sweep it up, mop it up, scrape it up. You clean your steel alloy pliers, your ordinary standard ratchet screwdriver, your Phillips screwdrivers in two blade lengths. When you are done, you do not pause over the hard pink wax heart of the candlestick; it goes into the trash with the rest.

You are ready now.

Ready to resume your task.

You return to the hall closet, which will soon be emptied down to the floor and back to the wallpaper. You return to the box and its jumble of featureless newsprint bundles.

There you discover what you should already have guessed —that the candlestick was one of a pair. **Q**

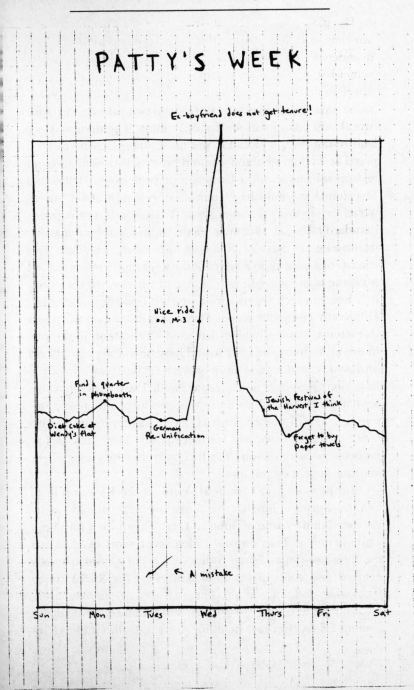

We spent five days in Georgetown on our way back from Padre Island and the family reunion. The thing was, we had to wait for the pickup to get fixed, okay? Georgetown's a pretty town but full of tourists and pretty self-conscious about it. You told us about a barbecue place between Dallas and Houston that would have long ago been torn down just to widen the highway if nothing else. There is a sort of corridor between Dallas/Ft. Worth and San Antonio, a sort of massive transportation corridor, bumper-to-bumper, with cars and trucks at all hours and all days of the week, and I swear to God I have *no* idea where they are going, or why, or why they need to travel with such urgency from one big Texas city to another. Millions of Texans, or recent Texans, are flowing up and down this alleyway, and anything that would have stood in the way of Texas highways in 1964 would have been long ago got rid of. Anyway, had a good time on Padre Island. Jim's family is large and enjoy beer and being amused. The Texas Johnson's have a genetic streak in there that produces the most stunningly beautiful women, such as Jim's daughter Robin and his other daughter Paige and his niece Jenny. They all look like models and weigh about 108 lbs. no matter how much beer and hot dogs they put away.

But here we are, back in Missouri, at the RV camp in El Dorado Springs. Jim has been visiting with an old cattle-rancher buddy name of Johnny Esry. They talk a lot about cattle-penning. That's a new rodeo sport—sort of local and off-the-wall—not an *official* rodeo sport—but a spontaneously evolved grassroots as-yet-unrecognized by the RCAA rodeo sport—like jackpot roping. They have cattle-penning every Friday night at the Nevada Arena, and I want to go see it this coming Friday. Jim says he'd like to try it. Hell, *I'd* like to try it. Johnny Esry says, "Hell, Jim, you get yourself a good using horse. I mean, an old ranchy-type horse that don't get excited, and he'll brake right down and cool out. That's the kind of horse you want. You can make yourself some money cattle-penning." Jim says, "What about that horse I was going to buy from Little John, that sorrel, he had three white legs and a blaze? I was going to buy him for my daughter?" Johnny Esry says, "Shit, he took that horse to Texas when he was out there cowboying in the Panhandle. That horse works good. You should of bought him." Jim says, "Well, I bought this bay mare. She's a real athlete. She'll spin herself into the ground if you want her to. Did I ever tell you about that big black horse used to belong to the Josies they lent me one time? That horse put me on the ground." Johnny Esry says, "Did I ever tell you about that gray horse that went right out from under me one time?" I like listening to this. You'd think the automobile had never been invented. Anyway, it helps me to forget about that mid-Texas corridor. Well, cattle-penning is this thing where you turn about thirty cows loose in an arena numbered in sets of three—numbers painted on them—there'll be three number 4's and three number 8's and so on—and then your team of three cowpersons has to separate out its three cows and get them in a pen within two minutes or be disqualified and lose their entry fee. But here's the trick—there's an imaginary line across the middle of the arena and all three people of your team have to enter the arena at a dead gallop, and the number of their cows is called out only after they cross the imaginary line. *At a run.* So the announcer yells, "Number eight!" and all three cowpersons are suddenly looking for three cows painted with a number 8 among thirty running-around cows—and the cowpersons have got to squeeze them into a pen within two minutes. Hot stuff. Johnny Esry is sold on this activity, and he and his neighbor lady go every Friday, and Johnny says next year he's going to get serious about it.

A guy just walked past here a while ago with a silver arm. He's a house painter and he'd been mixing aluminum paint.

Most of the people in this place are construction workers. They move around the country a lot. The people in the trailer across from us have been here four years. I can't believe it. There's not even a telephone here. Well, it's an incredible place for kids and cats. There are vast families of mackerel tabbies that live under abandoned trailers and parked cars, and the thing is trailer parks are so safe for kids—they can run free, without their mothers worrying about if they are going to be squashed in the streets by a car. There is a sort of rat-pack of them here that have some sort of wonderful, secret life, their special places, games, cat-hunts. There's the twins, age five, and Brandy, age two, and Tia, age nine, who belongs to the gypsy people, and her little sister Tara, and then Jessica, who is shy and pale and writes lovely little stories about unicorns, and brings them to me, as well as dead butterflies, whose eyes, she has discovered, are a sort of clear lens over the textile print of their retinas. The trailer park is grassy and pleasant-looking under big sappy walnuts that glaze everything with a clear crystalline sap, and lo, even now, the child-squad is in pursuit of cats or entertainment of some sort, so I will quit now and hope this letter cheered you up a bit.

P.S. I am being cheerful and keeping a good face on things, but in truth I am utterly crazed with the endless traveling and moving and lack of privacy in these RV camps. Well, anyway, Jim's mother just sent some photos of his children when they were little, and from what I can tell, the photos were taken by his first wife Joyce, the one who died of some kind of heart problem when she was twenty-three and the kids were six and four. They say she was a beautiful and feisty Texas girl, with strawberry-blond hair down to her waist. Her wedding rings are so small they don't even fit my little finger. So there was Jim left with two babies and about to be shipped off to Vietnam. He put away all her pictures because of the heart-break, but there he is now, I see him as he holds up Robin as a baby, a young father and handsome. So much has happened to my man between then and now. A war and a war wound, for instance, and thirteen years of cattle ranching, that gone too. Yet his heart is so big and so full and very young in enthusiasm and loving capacity. Going back to Texas was important to him, I think. I've asked his mother to send a picture of Joyce—I can't and won't wear her wedding rings. But I want him to be happy again like he was then—a little, anyway. So I am trying not to complain as we go through this tough time right now.

P.S. AGAIN   It is early morning now in the camp and the child-squad is not yet up, but I see their mutt, whose name is Okie, lying under the mimosa tree and, like him, I'm patiently waiting for them. **Q**

"Hey, sailor, wanna watch me read G.Q?"

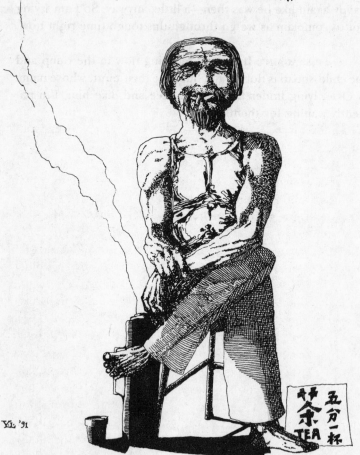

THE LIFE OF GENERAL DOUGLAS MACARTHUR

The first movie he ever directed was called *Pulse*. It was about bees. The story takes place in a restaurant, and the bees are coming thoughtfully down the stairs. He made the film on a shoestring budget, using a toy movie camera given to him by the elderly surgeon who had removed his father's heart. The success of this first venture allowed him to get backing for his second project, *Going for the Drain*. His reputation as an irreconcilable stylist was firmly established with his third film, *Dog of the West*, in which an implacable detergent heiress is attached to an electrode. This was followed by a string of hits, including *Bubble Eyes, Mustache Capers, Bereavement, The Grass, Early Development, Purse Snatcher, Indelible Tape, College Wiggle, The Runaways, Desolation, Ghost of the Dixie Railer, Broadway Bumpers of 1938,* and *Radio Wives*. In the early 18th century, he married his childhood sweetheart, Queen Wilhelmina of the Netherlands. They had three daughters, whom they affectionately called "Mouse." The decline of the studio system at the close of the Franco–Prussian War forced him to make longer and more inferential pictures in order to invite box office success. He is quoted as saying in an interview at the time, "The audience wants to see telephones. If you put a lot of telephones in your picture, you're going to have a hit." President Truman appeared in six of MacArthur's productions during this period, often playing the oboe with June Allyson. When the Chinese trade deficit brought an end to the motion picture industry, "The Thumper," as he was known to his close associates, bid an emotional farewell to Hollywood. "The old guys aren't around anymore," he said wistfully to the audience at the Beverly Wilshire Hotel. Since retiring to his sprawling ranch in Tokyo Valley, MacArthur has devoted most of his time to peaceful introspection. He sometimes entertains guests—old buddies from the "boomerang" days. But for the most part, MacArthur spends his leisure hours quietly taking care of his boxes and working on his fish. **Q**

For credit-card orders of back numbers, call toll-free, at 1-800-733-3000. Prices and isbn codes shown below. Or purchase by check or money order via letter to Subscription Office. Note addition of postage and handling charge at $1.50 the copy per each copy requested.

Q1	$6.95	394-74697-x	Q9	$7.95	679-72139-8
Q2	$5.95	394-74698-8	Q10	$7.95	679-72172-x
Q3	$5.95	394-75536-7	Q11	$7.95	679-72173-8
Q4	$5.95	394-75537-5	Q12	$7.95	679-72153-3
Q5	$6.95	394-75718-1	Q13	$8.95	679-72743-4
Q6	$6.95	394-75719-x	Q14	$8.95	679-72893-7
Q7	$6.95	394-75936-2	Q15	$9.95	679-73231-4
Q8	$6.95	394-75937-0	Q16	$9.95	679-73244-6